MURDER, MISCHIEF, AND MAYHEM

MURDER, MISCHIEF, AND MAYHEM

A PROCESS FOR CREATIVE RESEARCH PAPERS

W. KEITH KRAUS
Shippensburg State College

National Council of Teachers of English
1111 Kenyon Road, Urbana, Illinois 61801

Acknowledgments: I am indebted to Janie Lytle, Margie Finkey, and Sherry Smith, who typed the manuscript, as well as Professor Mark Givler, who proofread the final pages. And it goes without saying that without the enthusiastic response of students in my classes at Shippensburg State College this book could not have been published. Their eagerness for this project was only exceeded by their thoroughness, and I only hope the many hours they spent reading microfilm copies of old newspapers will make them better aware of the intricacies of research.

Staff Editor: Carol Schanche

Book Design: Tom Kovacs

NCTE Stock Number 32200

Library of Congress Cataloging in Publication Data

Main entry under title:

Murder, mischief, and mayhem.

   Includes bibliographies.
   1. Murder—United States—Case studies.   2. Research.
3. Report writing.   I. Kraus, W. Keith.
HV6524.M87   808'.023   78-9495
ISBN 0-8141-3220-0

CONTENTS

Introduction   1

THE PAPERS

Dr. Jacob Rosenzweig—Abortionist   7
  Vicki Bennett

The Criminal Career of Laura Fair   19
  Mark S. Daniel

The Bannock Indian War   31
  J. Kevin Hensel

The Execution of William Kemmler: The First Man to Die in the Electric Chair   42
  Barbara Hornbaker

The Last Bare Knuckle Prize Fight in America   51
  William Calaman

Reverend Hans Schmidt: Physician, Priest, Murderer   64
  Linda Trznadel

Grace Humiston, The First Woman Detective   75
  Tim McCarl

The Murder of Red Cassidy   92
  Vicki Kant

The Cocos Island Treasure Expeditions   103
  Grant Mahon

The Axe and Fire Murder of Major Everett S. Cofran   115
  Ralph Hultin

THE PROCESS

Guidelines for Researching and Writing about a Newspaper Case   131

  Library Research Exercises   131

  Preparation and Research   133

  Writing the Paper   137

  Mischief and Mayhem   142

An Annotated List of Topics   143

MURDER,
MISCHIEF,
AND MAYHEM

INTRODUCTION . . . OR
RESEARCH PAPERS DON'T BITE

This book is not meant to be simply another style manual for writing college research papers. There are plenty of those around and I don't really believe another one is needed. Rather, this text works under the assumption that freshman research and research papers can be interesting, an idea so heretical I'm almost afraid to advance it. Historically, the freshman research paper was never designed to be worthwhile or interesting in itself; it was, and alas still is in many cases, a trial balloon, a stepping stone, an exercise, a preparation for graduate school and beyond. At its zenith it is a means for scholars and scientists to communicate about original investigations, but at any lower level it is a dry run. In graduate school the research paper is written to prove that one can investigate and organize material just like a full-fledged member of the profession; in college it is to prove one is ready for graduate school (or as "practice for your other courses"); and on the high school level it is taught because "students will have to write research papers in college." (Perhaps for this reason English has come to be called a "service course.") It even results in a strange kind of praise for the exercise. When high schools ask former students what work in English has proved the most valuable, the research paper is invariably at the top of the list. Students without the high school experience are often in the position described by this bewildered freshman.

> My first day of class, I was told to hand in a 15-page analysis of two books at the end of the week. I got an F of course; the professor said the writing was *adequate* and the content *all right*, but the form was *all wrong*. I didn't know what he was talking about until a friend told me how to do footnotes and bibliographies.[1]

---

[1]Geraldine Allen, "What College Students Wish They'd Had in Senior English," *English Journal*, 53 (1964), 607.

So high schools teach the research paper as part of the college survival kit, and colleges see it as a survival kit for graduate school, and graduate schools hold that it is preparation for the time when a person undertakes original research. Thus, the high school research paper is really designed as training for laboratory research, although no one seems to see it that way. The stand taken in this book is that research can be interesting in its own right, that real research is indeed possible for freshmen, and that skills learned in doing a research paper can have immediate application.

Actually, the method presented here was developed out of the frustration I felt after reading a stack of badly done freshman research papers on *Moby Dick*. My papers were of the classic scissors-and-paste type with quotations lamely held together with weak transitional sentences interrupted by bad attempts at paraphrase. Or worse, I could tell that one book in the bibliography accounted for 90 percent of the paper, or still worse, the book wasn't *in* the bibliography. Or much worse, it probably came from the *Moby Dick* cheater sold by my friendly college bookstore.

The papers themselves were dull—"lacks a clear focus," "the transition is weak between sentences," "the style is too informal," "single space quotations over five lines,"—really dull. Of course I had a few good papers, but even they tended to be dull. It took me weeks to mark them, and I had to make up little correction games to force myself through the reading: "Today I'll read only papers in red plastic folders." But then I stumbled upon a clue.

I devised a series of library exercises to acquaint students with general reference works such as the *New York Times Index*, *The Readers' Guide*, *Book Review Digest*, etc. Not that I really planned to have my class use these sources in writing their papers, but I found that most freshmen have rarely used any reference other than *The Readers' Guide* and have a deeply rooted fear of a college library. My goal was to give them practical exposure to standard indexes and reference materials, acquaint them with our library's rapidly expanding micro-resources, and I suspect, salve my guilt in the course by teaching skills which might be useful in further college work.

The first exercise directed students to look up the *New York Times* on the day they were born and write a brief paragraph about what happened. Standard enough. They learned to use the microfilm machines and maybe noticed we carry the *Times* back to its first issue in 1851. Exercise two was designed to introduce the *Times Index* and the question was: "What were the circumstances surrounding the death of the following person?" And then each student was given a different name and date.

For years one of the fun books around our house has been a picture account of "the roaring twenties" which features close-ups of assorted gangsters riddled with bullets somewhere on Chicago's South Side. So for this question I lifted the obituary information on some of Capone's finest, put it on 3″ x 5″ cards (what else!), and dealt the cards out to the class, appropriately, face down. When the assignments were turned in, a number of students mentioned how interesting the story was surrounding their case, how strange that era must have been, and how different the account read compared to a "modern" newspaper story. We spent a few minutes in class joking about some of the mores of the 1920 gangster world they had uncovered, e.g., gold coffins, funeral processions through the "territory," the man's rivals uttering B movie eulogies. It was obvious this had been fun . . . for both of us. Looking up the review in *Book Review Digest* had been a chore, but the other was fun. Naturally, we forgot about all this when we turned to our "serious" project and everyone did his dull, badly done paper on *Moby Dick*. For the last time.

Before the next term began I spent a weekend in the library at the *Times Index* pulling out each volume, flipping to the "Murder" listings and noting the best cases dating from 1851. The kind of case I was looking for had to have certain qualities. First, it had to be a big enough case to allow students to pick and choose from the available

material, to select from a mass of information the key elements, facts, details, and quotations needed to construct a paper of about two thousand words. Second, I wanted cases that extended over a period of years in which new developments kept appearing and confusing the issue. This paper was going to be a legitimate test of a student's ability to research and organize scattered and chaotic materials. Third, I tried to pick cases that seemed to touch on some aspect of the American mind and character, that revealed a national or local attitude or strange custom of the time. For instance, one choice was the 1897 case of William Guldensuppe whose dismembered body was found over a course of three weeks, except for the head. His "remains," sans head, were put together and he was given an open casket funeral attended by thousands of curious viewers. Or again falling back on the gangster crimes, I selected the 1929 shooting of Red Cassidy in the Hotsy-Totsy Club in New York. Simply from the entries in the *Index* one can sense the flavor of the period, of gangland rivalries, police corruption, missing witnesses turning up in the East River.

Fourth, I picked only cases that looked interesting, somewhat bizarre, fun to read about and research . . . and to correct. No run-of-the-mill muggings, no domestic manslaughter cases, no same-day-confession crimes. I tried to find twenty-five "classics"—boy meets girl, boy accused of killing girl, boy released for lack of evidence, town lynches boy upon release, etc. But usually I had no idea how the crime turned out or really what it was all about, and no case was selected if it was so famous there were books about it (exit Leo Frank and Lizzie Borden). For all practical purposes, this was to be "original" research, or as close as one could get in a second term freshman course.

From the outset I knew I had scored with my fourth objective. The kids were really fascinated with their projects, and although some of their cases were often as complicated as *Moby Dick*, few people had trouble "understanding" what was going on. The greatest difficulty was organizing the material and putting it into a readable format. I found almost everyone had situations where facts were misstated, jumbled, or conflicting. In some cases the newswriting style was as foreign to students as an article in a scholarly journal. Students constantly had to look up archaic terms and "sic" seemed to be needed in almost every quotation. At first some people felt snowed under with material until they realized the importance of the proper selection of information; by degrees they began to realize that a story entitled "Police Continue Search for Killer" would offer little that was new and was hardly worth reading. (I was reminded of the typical comment I had heard on literary papers: "Every book says the same thing about *Moby Dick*, so what should I do?")

The papers themselves turned out to be the best I had ever received. They showed real hustle in the library and actual work in rewriting. A number of people found stories in papers other than the *Times*, and a few people discovered magazine articles concerning their murders. A couple of students had referred to encyclopedias or history books for general background material. To the best of my knowledge no paper was plagiarized, a fact I attribute to the students' interest in their topics (and, possibly, the fact that most of the news stories weren't written well enough to bother copying). There were no scissors-and-paste jobs; this may have been due to the built-in "narrative" structure and chronological progression of the cases. And most important of all, I enjoyed reading the papers . . . even the single-spaced quotations over five lines.

Since then I have refined and expanded the project somewhat. Recent topics have dealt with political scandals, espionage cases, biographies of minor "historical" figures, treasure hunts, and bare-knuckle prize-fights. Some of my best papers have been on Indian "uprisings," in which students were amazed to read contemporary accounts of "gallant horse soldiers dispatching copper-colored wretches" (Ute Indian War—1879), or how a group of Mormons used Indians to wipe out a wagon train of immigrants (Mountain Meadow Massacre—1857). I now allow students to pick their own topics or "areas" if they wish and I have a few takers; however, famous crimes is still the most popular category.

With this approach students often encounter unusual research problems, including strange terminology no longer in use. One student came across the term "arsenic eater" in his case and eventually discovered it was a practice for girls in the late 1800s to eat small amounts of arsenic to lighten their complexions. Also, news stories often contradict each other because in an era of sensational journalism each reporter tried to write the most revealing story possible using essentially the same facts. This forces students to be very evaluative in their research.

The research papers in this volume are the result of this kind of investigation. They were all written by students in freshman English Composition at Shippensburg State College and represent a small sample of the cases students in this class have researched in past years. A few of the murder cases are unsolved, and although they were sometimes more difficult to work with, students found them fascinating because it allowed them to formulate theories about what happened. (In fact, some of the solutions to murders are so ingenious, I'm convinced they've found the answer!) But even in those cases that are solved, I encourage students to write conclusions that are evaluative or speculative.

I chose these cases for inclusion as examples of well constructed research papers, but at the same time I tried to pick papers that are simply interesting to read by themselves. None of these "historical footnotes" has ever appeared in formal print and have generally been forgotten by time. I impress upon students the need for good quotations, statements that reflect the "temper of the times," and I think many of these papers fit that criterion. I have corrected the obvious typos and added a few marks of punctuation for the sake of clarity, but for all practical purposes, these papers are exactly as the students handed them in.

I should add that this approach is not a panacea and that not all my attempts are successful. Like everyone else, I receive papers that need a good proofreading or that lack continuity. A few people are unable to see the forest through the trees, and they spend pages recapping the predictable outcome of new trials and further appeals. A few times I was responsible for picking bad topics. Either they were too dull (Boston Police Strike) or else I tried to make the project too "literary" and it sank under its own weight. (One failure occurred when I assigned the story of the death of Floyd Collins in the Kentucky cave and asked the student to relate it to Robert Penn Warren's novel based on the episode. The paper might have worked for a senior English major, but for a freshman elementary student it was a disaster.)

At the end of the book I have included an annotated list of over 100 research topics that have resulted in superior papers for me, the cream of about 500 cases I have assigned in the last five years, along with some basic guidelines for assigning the topics. All of these assignments are workable and have enough material available to allow students to construct a research paper of about ten pages or more. Sometimes students can trace magazine articles written when the incident occurred, and a few cases are cited in books. Still, every attempt has been made to stay away from those cases which for all practical purposes have been "done" by other writers and prove nothing when students "rewrite" them.

Instructors who like this approach may wish to pick up *The Hutchinson Guide to Writing Research Papers* by Helene Hutchinson (Glencoe Press) and *Perception and Persuasion* by Raymond Paul and Pellegrino Goione (Crowell). These texts deal with the research paper in unusual ways and may suggest other ideas you can use. In any case, I hope this book gives you some fresh ideas so you'll never again be forced to read a dull and predictable research paper pasted together from critical books, or culled from a single "work." I really believe that once having tried this method you'll never go back to the *Moby Dick* casebook.

THE PAPERS

DR. JACOB ROSENZWEIG--ABORTIONIST

by Vicki Bennett

When a beautiful young girl was found stuffed in a trunk in a New York train depot in the summer of 1871, a new breed of murderer was exposed to the world. Young, vulnerable, unmarried mothers who, in the nineteenth century were so disgraced by their predicament they were desperate for any alternative, would seek out abortionists through coded advertisements in newspapers. Working under the pretense of helping women, these men actually endangered their lives. Every day in large cities girls died at the hands of these unscrupulous men and little was ever done about their deaths. Alice Augusta Bowlsby was one of these unfortunate victims. But when her mutilated body was found in a trunk in the Hudson River Train Depot, the crime became so sensational it touched off a three month search for her killer's identity and resulted in new laws to crack down on what was then termed the "evil of the age."

The nightmare began on August 26, 1871, when a small, horse-drawn furniture truck pulled into a train depot in New York City. It was driven by an old man, and its only contents were a small trunk. Immediately behind the truck, a one-horse coupé arrived with an elderly lady who got out, paid the driver, and sent him on his way. The woman then asked a young boy, who was standing nearby, to help unload the trunk from the van. In the process it was noticed the locks were not very secure, and the woman was concerned they would not stay closed with all the jostling and bouncing the trunk would receive on the long trip to

1

2

Chicago, its final destination. So the boy, who was called "Paddy,"[1] volunteered to find a rope and fasten it. After this was done, the old woman dismissed the truckman, but not before the observant Paddy noticed the name "Tripp" written on the side of the van.[2]

The trunk was then taken to the loading platform where it was thrown about and, as the lady had feared, the lid jarred loose. This would have passed unnoticed but porters noticed a terrible stench coming from the trunk. They decided to investigate the source of the odor and after the lid was cut open they found the doubled-up body of a beautiful young girl. Police were immediately summoned, and an Inspector Walling was put on the case.

The first person the Inspector questioned was the boy Paddy, who said the woman had gone down the street for something to eat, saying she would return in time for the train. However, she had not been seen since. Paddy did mention "Tripp" written on the side of the truck, so Walling sent men to search for any truck in the city with that name.

There was only one driver in the city with that name but he proved not to be the person who delivered the trunk; a man by the name of "Trapp" was found, but he denied he was ever at the depot that afternoon and Paddy said he was not the driver. The harried Inspector and his men worked all night to locate either "Tripp," the truck, or the old lady, and finally the driver of the coupé was found. He stated a woman had come that afternoon to hire him to take her to the depot, and he had obliged, but he could offer no other information. Still no leads turned up on the truck or driver, so police thought perhaps it came from

----

1. The boy's real name was Alexander Parks.

2. This name appears later in the case.

3

Brooklyn, Jersey City, or somewhere outside New York.

When the partially decomposed body was examined, it was revealed that death had occurred three days earlier. The heart, lungs, and brain were in a "healthy condition," but an opening in the abdominal cavity immediately led the Inspector to believe the trunk might have been taken from the "den of a New York abortionist."[3] There were many rumors as to the identity of the girl and one source hinted she was a young widow who had come to the city to seek "surgical relief" from a tumor in her stomach and had never returned home. Nothing was heard in the next few days, so this theory was assumed to be false. Inspector Walling searched his file of missing persons but could find no one who fit the girl's description. Many amateur detectives offered theories to the newspapers, but none made sense. One opinion was that the murder was committed by a woman and a burglar because it was thought that "no one but a woman would have left the body in such condition, and no man would have trusted a woman to dispose of the body."[4]

On the morning of August 28, 1871, the man who delivered the trunk was located. William Pickheit had read accounts in the paper about the murder and believed he was the man who had transported the trunk. At Police headquarters Pickheit related the following story to Captain Cameron of the 18th precinct:

> At 1 p.m. Saturday, a woman came to my stand and asked me to go to the basement of no. 687 2nd Avenue and get a trunk which I could obtain by ringing the bell and telling the people what I wanted. Then I was to put it on my truck and take it to the Hudson River Railroad Depot where she would be in a coupé.[5]

---

3. "The Trunk Mystery," New York Times, 28 August 1871, p. 8.

4. Ibid.

5. "Evil of the Age," New York Times, 29 August 1871, p. 8.

4

Pickheit said he went to the house and was led to a basement chamber. There he was met by several women and a tall man, whom he described so accurately that Acting Police Sergeant Rooney knew he was the infamous abortionist, Jacob Rosenzweig.

Sergeant Rooney put on street clothes and along with another officer went to No. 687 2nd Avenue. Rosenzweig's wife and daughter told the men the doctor was out so Rooney put the house under surveillance. He watched for Rosenzweig to arrive, and when he did he followed him into a liquor store near his house. He was about to arrest him when Rosenzweig recognized the officer and ran. But it was too late and after a brief struggle, Rooney got him into the waiting cab and took him to the station. Captain Cameron, who was also with Rooney when they went to the house, also brought in the servant girl from Rosenzweig's residence. Inspector Walling, who at that time had not heard the truckman's story, met the party and made Pickheit retell the incident. Paddy agreed to everything Pickheit said, except for a minor detail of shaking hands with the woman when they parted.

When Rosenzweig was asked if he knew anything about the trunk which he had allegedly given to Pickheit, he appeared "perfectly amazed" at the question and denied ever having set eyes on him. Pickheit believed Rosenzweig to be the man who had given him the trunk, but he was not sure he had ever seen the servant girl before. The wife had been in the basement at the time, but Pickheit remembered her asking him where he was taking the trunk. However, Mrs. Rosenzweig was contacted and denied all knowledge of the business and declared she was "too delicate to be downstairs on Saturday when the truckman called."[6]

---

6. "Evil of the Age," p. 8.

5

At this point Inspector Walling was still completely baffled as to the identity of the girl and the woman in the coupé. He looked for clues in Rosenzweig's house and also at a house in Amity Place which was said to be occupied by Rosenzweig and used for unlawful abortions. At the second address some papers were found in his desk, including an advertisement apparently taken from the New York Times which read: "Ladies in trouble; guaranteed immediate relief, sure and safe; no fees required until perfectly satisfied. Dr. Ascher, Amity Place."[7] A death certificate for a stillborn child was also found and Rosenzweig's name appeared as the doctor of record.

Meanwhile, even though the condition of the body was known and the odor unbearable, hundreds of people came to view the unfortunate girl. It was hoped that someone would recognize her, but for the most part people came out of simple curiosity.[8]

An undertaker, James F. Boyle, added more evidence when he showed up at the jail and asked to see Rosenzweig. When he looked at the prisoner, he exclaimed: "yes, that's the man!" and went on to make an interesting statement.

> That man came into my store and asked how much it would cost to bury a woman. He said she was a servant of his who had died. I asked him for a certificate from the doctor, to get a permit from the Board of Health and he said that the doctor wasn't available. Then he left.[9]

———————————————

7.   "The Trunk Mystery," New York Times, 30 August 1871, p. 8.

8.   The New York Times cautioned that "viewing would be allowed, although decomposition was rapidly progressing, and the remains are becoming dangerous to the health of the hospital and vicinity." Ibid.

9.   "The Trunk Mystery," Philadelphia Inquirer, 30 August 1871, p. 6.

6

When confronted with this witness Rosenzweig replied: "Yes, I wash dar, but I just makes fun."[10]

Finally, on August 30, 1871, the identity of the murdered girl was uncovered. She was found to be Miss Alice Augusta Bowlsby, 20 years old, from Patterson, New Jersey. Dr. Theodore Kinne of New Jersey had visited the morgue, examined the remains, and thought he recognized a scar on the left arm where he had once vaccinated Miss Bowlsby. Dr. Kinne left and returned with Dr. Joseph F. Parker, a dentist, and after a full examination, Parker said he recognized his dental work "beyond the possibility of mistake." The doctors revealed that Miss Bowlsby had left her aunt's home in Newark to go to her home in Patterson by way of New York. Still, friends of Miss Bowlsby claimed it was impossible the murdered girl was Alice. She was described as a young girl "whose life had never been darkened, and upon whom the breath of suspicion never fallen."[11] They said she lived in a respectable society and had an "amiable character, elegant manners, and good conversational powers."[12]

In hope of turning up clues relevant to this new information, Inspector Walling ordered another search of Rosenzweig's house--this time he looked for an article of clothing or something that could have belonged to Miss Bowlsby. Nothing was found until police inspected the kitchen. There, in several wash tubs, were clothes the servant girl had been washing, including a linen handkerchief which seemed to bear lettering. When taken back to the stationhouse and placed under a

----

10. Ibid.

11. "Trunk Mystery," Philadelphia Inquirer, 1 September 1871, p. 4.

12. Ibid.

7

magnifying glass the officer saw "distinct characters sentencing the monster Rosenzweig to the fullest penalty of his crime."[13] For embroidered on the handkerchief was the name "A. A. Bowlsby."

A further search of the house produced more incriminating evidence. Cards bearing addresses of other patients, papers that proved Rosenzweig's identity, and several much used abortionist's instruments were uncovered. But still the identity of the old woman who had consigned the trunk to the train depot was unknown.[14] When questioned again Paddy still stuck to his story that someone had shaken hands with the unidentified woman accomplice. Another truckman was found who had been on the same corner with Pickheit and stated that a few minutes after Pickheit left for the trunk a man approached him and asked if he had been engaged to take a trunk to the depot. He answered that Pickheit was the man he wanted, but he had just gone. Now police believed that this person was the mysterious "Tripp," and that with a woman accomplice, he had taken Alice Bowlsby to the abortionist.[15]

On the morning of September 1, 1871, a lady drove up to the stationhouse in a carriage. She was shown to Captain Cameron's private room and they had a long talk.[16] She proved to be Harriet Williams, the aunt of Alice Bowlsby. She stated that from what she knew of her niece's habits Walter F. Conklin was probably the man responsible for Alice's

---

13. "The Terrible Crime," New York Times, 31 August 1871, p. 8.

14. Inspector Walling, however, boasted he did not need the woman, and said that sometime when he "had nothing to do he would look for her." "Evil of the Age," New York Times, 1 September 1871, p. 8.

15. It was later decided that Paddy did not actually see the name "Tripp" on the van, but rather the woman accomplice mentioned that particular name.

16. Since the case was closed to Inspector Walling's satisfaction, he left town for a rest and Captain Cameron took over the case.

8

"misfortune." Conklin had visited her at her aunt's house three days before her departure. Conklin was known to have gone to New York on August 26 and returned the same night. Thus, suspicion grew that he was the "Tripp" involved in the case. Police went immediately to the silk mill where Walter Conklin worked, but a few hours before newspapers printed the story and police arrived too late. Walter Conklin had committed suicide.

On October 25, 1871, the case of Jacob Rosenzweig came up in court. He was charged with manslaughter by medical malpractice, and even though a long period of time had elapsed since the incident, the courtroom was full. The District Attorney began with the statement that the prisoner was guilty of one of the "highest crimes known to law," yet could only be punished in the state prison for seven years. In response the defense offered that "the period had arrived when, as the prisoner believed, the cloud which had rested on his reputation would be cleared away . . . when, in the temple of justice, away from public clamor, he would be declared not guilty."[17]

The emotional trial lasted only a few days. District Attorney Garvin described the situation as that of a young girl "ruined and betrayed; a child of misfortune, she was stricken down with the thought that every day brought her nearer to disgrace. . . ."[18] When Rosenzweig took the stand he denied participation in any abortion, and though eight witnesses testified favorably in regard to his character, the case made

----

17. "The Trunk Mystery," New York Times, 28 October 1871, p. 1.

18. "The Trunk Mystery," New York Times, 29 October 1871, p. 1.

9

by the prosecution was too strong.[19]   On October 28, 1871, the jury,
after only one hour and fifty minutes of deliberation, found Jacob
Rosenzweig guilty of causing the death of Alice A. Bowlsby and sentenced
him to seven years imprisonment with hard labor.

Yet even with Rosenzweig's conviction many unanswered questions
remained. Who was the unnamed woman assistant? Was Walter Conklin the
father of the unborn child, or did he simply introduce Alice to the
abortionist? Probably no one will ever know the real truth about this
incident, but it is hypothesized by the author of this paper that Walter
Conklin was the man who fathered Alice's unborn child. Because being
pregnant and unmarried was such a stigma in those days, something had
to be done about the baby. Conklin must have read Rosenzweig's advertisement in the paper and gone to New York to look into the matter. He
had no intention of getting Alice killed, but simply paid Rosenzweig to
perform the abortion. Alice then went to New York with Conklin posing
as "Mr. and Mrs. Tripp." Then when the girl died, "Tripp" and Rosenzweig arranged for the body to be transported to Chicago for disposal in
some way. When Conklin learned in the papers that he had been uncovered
he killed himself.

Because of this case the District Attorney went before the New
York legislature to have death by abortion changed to murder rather than
manslaughter. Arguing that the "crime strikes at the root of all
civilized society," he succeeded in convincing the legislature to
extend the penalty to twenty years--and inadvertently this allowed

---

19. To refute the character witnesses, Garvin brought out that
Rosenzweig had been a saloon keeper until he purchased a $40 diploma
from a school in Philadelphia to "pursue his murderous calling."
"Rosenzweig's Medical Diploma," New York Times, 5 September 1871, p. 3.

10

Rosenzweig to go free. In February, 1873, Rosenzweig was granted a new
trial because the law now made his sentence questionable. The presiding
judge then ruled that his case could not be tried under the new law and
so, two years after the crime, the murderer of Alice Augusta Bowlsby was
released.[20]

Alice Bowlsby was not the first woman to die in this horrible manner, and perhaps her death did little to diminish this illegal practice
in her day. Many men like Rosenzweig performed similar "services" in
New York, and most operations went undiscovered until an innocent victim
was killed. There was an investigation because of the notoriety of this
case, and the law was changed to extend the penalty for such a crime,
but one suspects there was little general reform. Today laws are such
that women can have legal abortions, so legislation has effectively
eliminated this kind of crime. But for Alice Bowlsby, and countless
other girls, the laws came too late to protect them from men who were
justly described as "insensitive villains."

---

20. On February 17, 1873, Rosenzweig wrote a letter to the editor
of the New York Times in which he pleaded for compassion as a "Polander"
and stated: "God knows that I am not the man who committed the terrible
deed." The editor called him a "scoundrel and a quack."

11

WORKING BIBLIOGRAPHY

"Case of Rosenzweig Reviewed by a Lawyer." New York Times, 31 October 1871, p. 1.

"Danger of His Escape." New York Times, 10 February 1873, p. 4.

"Evil of the Age." New York Times, 29 August 1871, p. 8.

"Evil of the Age." New York Times, 1 September 1871, p. 8.

"Evil of the Age." New York Times, 2 September 1871, p. 8.

Rosenzweig, Jacob. "Letter to The New York Times." New York Times, 14 February 1873, p. 6.

"Rosenzweig." New York Times, 29 October 1871, p. 1.

"Rosenzweig." New York Times, 8 October 1872, p. 5.

"Rosenzweig." New York Times, 26 November 1872, p. 8.

"Rosenzweig Case, The." New York Times, 28 September 1873, p. 3.

"Rosenzweig Case, The." New York Times, 13 November 1873, p. 5.

"Rosenzweig Case, The." New York Times, 14 November 1873, p. 3.

"Rosenzweig Case, The." New York Times, 12 December 1873, p. 8.

"Rosenzweig's Medical Diploma." New York Times, 5 September 1871, p. 3.

"Rosenzweig the Abortionist--His Fruitless Attempt to Get Out on Bail." New York Times, 8 September 1871, p. 2.

"Rosenzweig's Trial." New York Times, 26 October 1871, p. 2.

"Rosenzweig's Trial." New York Times, 27 October 1871, p. 22.

"Terrible Crimes, The." New York Times, 31 August 1871, p. 8.

"Terrible Mystery, A." New York Times, 27 August 1871, p. 1.

"Trunk Tragedy." New York Times, 3 September 1871, p. 8.

"Trunk Mystery, The." New York Times, 28 August 1871, p. 8.

"Trunk Mystery, The." New York Times, 30 August 1871, p. 8.

"Trunk Mystery, The." New York Times, 2 September 1871, p. 8.

12

"Trunk Mystery, The." New York Times, 28 October 1871, p. 1.

"Trunk Mystery, The." New York Times, 29 October 1871, p. 1.

"Trunk Mystery." Philadelphia Inquirer, 30 August 1871, p. 6.

"Trunk Mystery." Philadelphia Inquirer, 31 August 1871, p. 6.

"Trunk Mystery." Philadelphia Inquirer, 1 September 1871, p. 4.

THE CRIMINAL CAREER OF LAURA FAIR

by Mark S. Daniel

It is an old saying that the female of the species is deadlier than the male and such a maxim was never more true than in the case of Mrs. Laura Fair. With her accomplishments of killing one man, shooting another, swindling her doctor, and attempting to poison the judge who convicted her, Mrs. Fair would certainly seem to qualify as one of the most determined criminals in American history. But in addition she was a public lecturer on "morals, virtue, and reform," and was alternately defended and damned by the papers of the time. Her bizarre "career" was such that one newspaper editor, upon hearing she might be leaving her native California, believed that "with loss of such a shepherdess [that state would return] to a second Garden of Eden, where the peaceful and pastoral virtues [might] again take root. . . ."[1]

Laura Fair (nee Hunt) was born in New Orleans in 1836, but after her marriage to William Stone the couple moved to California. The first of four marriages ended in divorce when she charged her husband with mental cruelty and physical abuse. Stone countercharged that his wife had received "gentlemanly attentions" from a Mr. Grayson, and the fact that Laura married Grayson soon after her divorce would seem to support this charge.

After a second divorce Laura married Mr. William Fair, a successful attorney, who, after only a short time "blew his brains out" in San

---

1. "Laura D. Fair Delivers a Lecture," New York Times, 27 January 1873, p. 1.

1

2

Francisco in 1860.[2] Shortly thereafter, Mrs. Fair moved to Virginia

City, Nevada, and operated a boarding house with the help of a male

partner. After the partner insisted on raising Old Glory over their

establishment in spite of Laura's protestations, Mrs. Fair shot and

wounded him.[3] It was at this point that she met her lover/victim: the

Honorable A. P. Crittenden. Crittenden defended her case and won it.

Crittenden was the nephew of the U.S. Senator to Kentucky and had

graduated from West Point in the same class as Generals Beauregard and

Sherman in 1835.[4] As a junior partner in the firm of Wilson and Crit-

tenden, he became prosperous as a result of the firm's specialization

in land deals. The couple's romance was only briefly interrupted when

Laura married a man named Snyder, whom she rapidly left, without legal

process, after she accused him of adultery.[5] Free of Snyder, Mrs. Fair

became Crittenden's mistress and made no attempt to conceal that fact.

Later, when Crittenden, acting on friends' advice, tried to end the

affair, Laura threatened to kill herself and several times afterward,

the lawyer had to dissuade her from rash action.[6]

On the evening of November 3, 1870, Crittenden met his family, who

had just returned from a trip, and boarded the ferry El Capitan to cross

San Francisco Bay to go home. A few minutes after the boat started out

a veiled woman dressed in black appraoched the seated Crittenden,

---

2. "Fair-Crittenden Tragedy," New York Times, 8 April 1871, p. 6.

3. Mrs. Fair was an ardent Southern sympathizer.

4. Ibid.

5. "A Murderess on the Witness Stand," Philadelphia Inquirer,
7 April 1871, p. 1.

6. "Fair-Crittenden Tragedy," p. 6.

3

levelled a pistol at the lawyer and shot him in the chest--all without saying a word.[7]

Captain Kentzal of the Harbor Police happened to be on board and was summoned to the scene. With a description of the woman, Kentzal, accompanied by Parker Crittenden, went off on the trail of the attacker.[8] While the two were searching, Crittenden's wife and daughter made the comatose lawyer more comfortable by placing his head in his wife's lap and giving him brandy through his clenched teeth. After only a few minutes of searching, Kentzal and Parker found the veiled woman in one of the ferry's cabins. When the younger Crittenden identified her as his father's assaultress, the woman averred: "I did shoot him," and added, "I meant to kill him."[9]

When the boat docked, Captain Kentzal and the authorities took the woman, now formally identified as Mrs. Laura D. Fair, to the San Francisco stationhouse where she exhibited odd mannerisms, supposedly to feign insanity. At first, the symptoms were ignored; however, when Mrs. Fair appeared on the verge of doing herself harm, "a physician was called, and an opiate administered. . . . It was given to her in a glass, and she committed the unladylike act of biting a piece out of the tumbler."[10] While under the influence of the heavy dosage, Mrs. Fair repeatedly called Crittenden's name--"as if to call him to her side."[11]

---

7. Another source had her shouting, "You have ruined me and my child." "The Fair-Crittenden Tragedy," New York Times, 8 April 1871, p. 6.

8. Parker Crittenden was A. P. Crittenden's son.

9. "The San Francisco Tragedy," New York Times, 13 November 1870, p. 3.

10. "San Francisco Tragedy," p. 3.

11. "The Fair-Crittenden Tragedy," New York Times, 8 April 1871, p. 6.

4

A. P. Crittenden was taken to his house and "lingered in great agony" for three days, but on November 6, 1870, he died from the wound in his right lung.[12]

At her trial Laura Fair declared herself an ardent advocate of free love.[13] Stating her marriage to Snyder to be invalid because there was no love between them, Laura then swore she was Crittenden's "true wife in the sight of God" because their love "transcended legal documentation."[14]

In rebuttal, the prosecution introduced "evidence, showing her character to be notoriously bad before she met Crittenden. . . . Over one hundred letters [of correspondence] were published . . . many others . . . unfit for publication."[15] Other testimony "proved that she had stated some time before the murder that he [Crittenden] should die."[16,17] After all the evidence was in, the jury made its decision on April 26, 1871--guilty as charged of murder in the first degree.

Laura Fair remained in the public eye in the days spanning her conviction and her June 3 sentencing as rumors of her suicide were mingled with a report of her bilking her physician out of $2100 in

---

12. "Treasure Shipments--Murders--Movements of Vessels," *Philadelphia Inquirer*, 5 November 1870, p. 1.

13. "Murderess on the Witness Stand," p. 1.

14. *Ibid*.

15. "The Crittenden Murder Trial," *Philadelphia Inquirer*, 13 April 1871, p. 1.

16. "The Trial of Mrs. Fair," *Philadelphia Inquirer*, 30 March 1871, p. 1.

17. Mrs. Fair did more than threaten; she had shot at him two years before but had missed. ("S.F. Tragedy," p. 1.)

5

fees.[18,19] A Dr. Trasks attempted to seize Laura's assets but it was discovered her mother had previously withdrawn the funds.[20] A few days before her sentence, a <u>Chicago Tribune</u> reporter gained access to the murderess and interviewed her in her cell. When he bluntly asked her preference between life imprisonment and being hanged, Mrs. Fair bitterly swore "for her daughter's sake, she would rather die, that the girl might 'go away and the stain after a while, would be forgotten.'"[21] On June 3, 1871, Judge Dwinell sentenced Mrs. Fair to be hanged on July 28 of that year. The murderess took the news calmly, while a group of feminists in the gallery protested the punishment and comforted Mrs. Fair's mother.[22]

But this sentence did not stick, however, for the state supreme court granted her a new trial on the basis of the violation of her rights in the proceedings.[23] On September 26, 1872, almost two years after the crime, Mrs. Fair received a retrial. Both counsels virtually re-enacted the first trial and introduced no new evidence whatsoever. After both sides reiterated their cases, the jury retired to their chambers. The

---

18. "Railway Construction--the Murderess--etc." <u>Philadelphia Inquirer</u>, 29 April 1871, p. 4.

19. "Telegraphic Brevities," <u>New York Times</u>, 17 May 1871, p. 1.

20. Later, Mrs. Fair was in turn cheated by her own mother, who deposited the money in her own account and refused to return it to her daughter. ("Mrs. Fair Files Suit against Her Mother," <u>New York Times</u>, 23 January 1872, p. 2.)

21. "Putting Prisoners to the Torture," Editorial. <u>New York Times</u>, 17 September 1871, p. 4.

22. "Mrs. Laura D. Fair Sentenced to Be Hanged," <u>New York Times</u>, 4 June 1871, p. 1.

23. Mrs. Fair's attorney was somehow not permitted to make a closing statement, and evidence had been allowed of her "former bad character for chastity." ("New Trial for Mrs. Fair," <u>New York Times</u>, 6 February 1872, p. 1.

6

next day, when the jury requested additional guidance on what consti-
tuted proof of insanity, "the court instructed them that unless the
evidence introduced for the purpose of showing insanity [was] sufficient
to overcome the presumption of sanity, it [was] not sufficient."[24]

At 9 a.m. on September 30, after sixty hours of deliberation, the
jury awarded a verdict of acquittal to the defendant, who promptly
fainted.

Public reaction to the "extraordinary verdict of acquittal" was
immediate and blustery.

> The verdict excites no surprise, on account of the
> inferior character of the jury, the members of which were
> selected . . . from among men so ignorant as not to know
> enough about this notorious case to have formed any opinion
> favorable or unfavorable to the prisoner.[25]

Another writer fumed: "Such a verdict could have no other inter-
pretation but this, that in California adultery is no crime, and that a
wanton is justified in taking the life of her accomplice. . . ."[26] In
the same vein, an editorial entitled "Balking Justice" (New York Times,
October 1, 1872, p. 1.) abrasively castigated the system of justice for
its complacency in allowing itself to be used to delay sentence and
procure public exposure for people involved. The author condemned the
Supreme Court for allowing a retrial on no new evidence and berated
judicial figures in general by calling all "judges nowadays . . . weak,
wavering, without dignity, without authority." San Francisco voiced its
opinion with this declaration: "The press of this city and state

---

24. "The Laura Fair Trial--Jury Out," Philadelphia Inquirer, 30
September 1872, p. 1.

25. "Mrs. Fair Acquitted--the California Jury System," New York
Times, 1 October 1872, p. 1.

26. "Case of Laura D. Fair," Editorial, Philadelphia Inquirer, 28
November 1872, p. 4.

7

denounce the verdict in the Fair case as a mockery of justice."[27]
Still another Californian commentator sarcastically "congratulated [San
Francisco] on the vindication of law, morality, and decency in the re-
sult of the trial."[28]

Again, as after her conviction, Laura refused to keep out of the
limelight; instead, she embarked on a post-trial escapade nearly rival-
ling her pre-murder days in news content. Adjudged innocent of her
"crime," Mrs. Fair undertook to recover her property: a Sharps four-
barrelled pistol found at the scene of the Crittenden slaying. For some
reason the police refused to return the item.[29] One of Mrs. Fair's con-
temporaries acidly remarked: "A California jury has just given her free
license to slay whomsoever she listeth, and now the California police
seek to thwart her in the exercise of this gentle prerogative by with-
holding the means of enforcing it."[30]

At this point Mrs. Fair decided to take up a more conventional form
of notoriety and announced she would give a public lecture entitled
"Wolves in the Fold." But shortly before she was to leave for the
lecture hall, a crowd gathered around her residence and tried to storm
the house. Mrs. Fair's requests for a police escort were refused by the
police chief and a small group of friends attended Laura in an upstairs
room during the commotion, until, after two hours of catcalls and jeers,

27. "Opinions on the Fair Case," Philadelphia Inquirer, 2 October
1872, p. 1.

28. "The Acquittal of Mrs. Fair," New York Times, 1 October 1872,
p. 4.

29. "Mrs. Fair Demands Return of Pistol," New York Times, 14
November 1872, p. 4.

30. Ibid.

8

the crowd dispersed.[31]   Once again, the press had a field day, substi-
tuting vitriol for ink in their pens:

> The tumult at San Francisco which was sufficient to
> prevent the notorious Laura D. Fair from delivering a
> lecture upon a subject chosen by herself, may be looked
> upon as a protest against defects in the administration
> of criminal law. . . . If the mob in San Francisco desires
> justly to testify its feelings against the persons who are
> responsible in this affair, it should go beyond Jesabel
> [sic], who has profited by it.[32]

Not until January 26 did Laura Fair fulfill her desire to speak.
Because of the inavailability of a lecture hall, Laura rented a Sacra-
mento bar, and when she discovered her admission cost kept her audience
away she opened the lecture to free admission and soon had a full
house.[33]

Soon after her debut as a speaker, a waiter named "Frank" implicated
her in a plot to poison Judge Dwinell.[34]   The man claimed Mrs. Fair
attempted to persuade him to add poison to the milk can on the judge's
porch and revealed the plot was devised before her retrial.[35]

On a lower level of revenge Laura proceeded to take out the frustra-
tions built up by the trial press on a "luckless charicaturist"--George
Thistleton--who had drawn unflattering sketches of her during the

---

31. "Mrs. Fair--Not Allowed to Lecture," New York Times, 22
November 1872, p. 1.

32. "Case of Laura D. Fair," p. 4.

33. "Laura D. Fair Delivers a Lecture," New York Times, 27 January
1873, p. 1.

34. "Plot Discovered to Poison the Judge Who Convicted Her," New
York Times, 23 November 1872, p. 8.

35. The plot was later written off as the machinations of the
waiter, who was thought to be insane.

9

proceedings.[36] Though the press threw their support behind the artist
and "favored her with an almost unanimous suggestion that she be hung
[sic], she took no notice of it. . . ."[37]

The final entry in the tragicomic saga of Laura Fair was a wry
comment on the consistency of the lady's moral fibre. The author of an
editorial sharply chastised Mrs. Fair's "Hard-hearted attorney" for
actually trying to collect his fees, which the lady refused to pay.[38]
The "unreasonable wretch" went so far as to force the "persecuted and
exasperated" Mrs. Fair into a court suit to get the $2900 in question;
having succeeded at that, he then burdened her with court costs.[39] To
add to Mrs. Fair's woes, a second member of her defense team began to
threaten to sue for his fees. The author concluded by stating he would
not be shocked if she "either shot her tormentors or deprived California
of the honor of her residence."[40]

In retrospect there should be no doubt about Laura Fair's guilt;
the verdict of her first trial was accurate. The only disputable area
was the defendant's mental condition--was Laura Fair a psychopathic
killer or did she escape the gallows by merely pretending to be insane?

Mrs. Fair's behavior prior to the murder would give weight to the
argument that the lady was not in control of herself. The circumstances
of her first divorce were tangled with charges and countercharges; was
William Stone the ogre Laura made him out to be, or were his cruelties

36. "Mrs. Fair Institutes a Libel Suit," New York Times, 6 January
1873, p. 4.

37. "Minor Topics," New York Times, 6 January 1873, p. 1.

38. "Minor Topics," New York Times, 23 June 1873, p. 4.

39. Ibid.

40. Ibid.

10

mere figments of fantasy? The rapid changeover in her marriage partners
would seem to indicate a character disorder preventing her from main-
taining a close relationship with one person for any length of time.

Another view might be that Mrs. Fair's behavior resulted from a
lack of maturity. The infantile determination to have things go her
way could provoke her to violence when conflicts arose. An example of
this was the Virginia City incident, which resulted from a petty
argument.

Laura's compulsion for revenge was an important factor in her
career; the actions against a photographer, a newspaper cartoonist, her
business partner, Judge Dwinell, and her lover prove it. In Crittenden's case, motive was ample: loss of his love, loss of his money,
anger over having been used and discarded, as well as anger toward the
woman who had taken away her lover. Coupled with Mrs. Fair's mental
state, these reasons might have been enough to set off her murderous
instincts.

In the category of generally bizarre behavior, the facts again
point to Laura's basic instability. First, she shot Crittenden in
public, in front of his family and any other witnesses present; then,
once in custody, she made no attempt to deny the accusation of her crime
but proclaimed her desire to kill him instead. During her trial, her
testimony of her affiliation with free love ideals did little to dissuade
the public from judging her insane. The absurdity of the woman sermon-
izing about "Wolves in the Fold" speaks for itself. If Crittenden's
murderess was sane, the only possible conclusion would be Laura Fair was
utterly ruthless, using whatever means necessary to succeed, including
murder and a convincing and extremely protracted mime of madness.

11

WORKING BIBLIOGRAPHY

"Acquittal of Mrs. Fair, The." New York Times, 1 October 1872, p. 4.

"Balking Justice." Editorial. New York Times, 8 February 1872, p. 4.

"By Mail & Telegraph." New York Times, 13 March 1873, p. 1.

"Case of Laura D. Fair." Editorial. Philadelphia Inquirer, 28 November 1872, p. 4.

"Crittenden's Murderess Acquitted." Philadelphia Inquirer, 1 October 1872, p. 1.

"Crittenden Murder Trial, The." Philadelphia Inquirer, 13 April 1871, p. 1.

"Fair-Crittenden Tragedy, The." New York Times, 8 April 1871, p. 6.

"Fair Laura Again, The." Philadelphia Inquirer, 6 January 1873, p. 1.

"Fair Libel, The." Philadelphia Inquirer, 7 January 1873, p. 1.

"Laura D. Fair Delivers a Lecture." New York Times, 27 January 1873, p. 1.

"Laura Fair Trial--Jury Out." Philadelphia Inquirer, 30 September 1872, p. 1.

"Laura Fair." New York Times, 8 June 1872, p. 1.

"Minor Topics." Editorial. New York Times, 6 January 1873, p. 4.

"Minor Topics." Editorial. New York Times, 23 June 1873, p. 4.

"Mrs. Fair Acquitted--the California Jury System." New York Times, 1 October 1872, p. 1.

"Mrs. Fair Convicted of Murder in First Degree." New York Times, 27 April 1871, p. 1.

"Mrs. Fair Demands Return of Pistol." New York Times, 14 November 1872, p. 4.

"Mrs. Fair Files Suit against Her Mother." New York Times, 23 January 1872, p. 2.

"Mrs. Fair Institutes a Libel Suit." New York Times, 6 January 1873, p. 1.

12

"Mrs. Fair--Not Allowed to Lecture." <u>New York Times</u>, 22 November 1872,
    p. 1.

"Mrs. Laura D. Fair Sentenced to Be Hanged." <u>New York Times</u>, 4 June
    1871, p. 1.

"Murderess on the Witness Stand, A." <u>Philadelphia Inquirer</u>, 7 April
    1871, p. 2.

"New Orleans Reminiscence, A--Her First Divorce, Sixteen Years Ago."
    <u>New York Times</u>, 18 July 1871, p. 1.

"New Trial for Mrs. Fair." <u>New York Times</u>, 6 February 1872, p. 1.

"Not Allowed to Lecture." <u>New York Times</u>, 22 November 1872, p. 1.

"Opinions of the Fair Case." <u>Philadelphia Inquirer</u>, 2 October 1872,
    p. 1.

"Putting Prisoners to the Torture." Editorial. <u>New York Times</u>, 17
    September 1871, p. 4.

"Plot Discovered to Poison the Judge Who Convicted Her." <u>New York
    Times</u>, 23 November 1872, p. 8.

"Promise of Lecture." Editorial. <u>New York Times</u>, 20 November 1872,
    p. 4.

"Railway Construction--the Murderess--etc." <u>Philadelphia Inquirer</u>, 29
    April 1871, p. 4.

"San Francisco Tragedy, The." <u>New York Times</u>, 13 November 1870, p. 3.

"Telegraphic Brevities." <u>New York Times</u>, 17 May 1871, p. 1.

"Treasure Shipments--Murders--Movements of Vessels." <u>Philadelphia
    Inquirer</u>, 5 November 1870, p. 1.

"Trial of Mrs. Fair, The." <u>Philadelphia Inquirer</u>, 30 March 1871, p. 1.

THE BANNOCK INDIAN WAR

by J. Kevin Hensel

Perhaps the longest-running conflict in the history of the United
States was between the American Indian and the white man. The problem
existed when the first colonies were established in Virginia and New
England and continued to confront the nation until the twentieth century. But the conflict reached a climax during the twenty-year period
following the American Civil War, culminating in a series of wars in
which the Indian way of life was destroyed forever. The Bannock War,
fought in areas of Southern Idaho, Eastern Oregon, and Western Montana
during the spring and summer of 1878, was small when compared with
other Indian wars of the same decade such as the Nez Percé War,[1] but it
adequately portrayed the hopelessness of the Indian struggle. It was
a typical Indian war, fought in a typical fashion, with an all too
typical conclusion--the forced acceptance of the reality of reservation
life by the Indians.

The Bannock War came as no great shock to the Northwest, for events
leading up to it gave a clear indication of what was to follow, and the
specific causes of the conflict only ignited violence that had been
dormant there for some time. The relentless attack of white civilization in the 1870s took the Indian's last vestige of homeland and left
him without any place to run.[2] A newspaper editorial at the time summed

---

1. The Nez Percé War took place in the same general area during
1877, but was somewhat greater in scale.

2. "The Indians of the North-west," Editorial, New York Times, 12
July 1878, p. 4.

1

2

up the position as "the 'irrepressible conflict' between their [the Indians'] roving mode of life and the demands for strictly prescribed bounds made by civilization leading to a final struggle in that region [the Northwest], before the red race, hopelessly worsted [sic], sinks beneath the power of the white."[3]   General Sherman summed up the situation in a fiercer context: "There is no help for it; the Indians must conform or be driven, like the Nez Percés, far away to the buffalo region or, if they prefer it, to their happy hunting ground."[4]   The war was indeed no surprise for many whites in Oregon who, as evidenced by this statement by Agent Rooke of the Klamath Indian Agency, eagerly awaited an Indian confrontation: "There seems to be a determination on the part of many white people to have war here, cause or no cause."[5] This then was the general situation the Indians of the Northwest faced in the fall and winter of 1877, when other problems of a more specific nature began to appear.

At this time the Bannock Indians of Idaho were confined and dependent upon the government for food and clothing. Reduced to a tribe of six hundred,[6] they were not allowed to send out hunting parties and had to rely upon their agent for supplies, which were totally inadequate. The Bannocks received four pounds of meat per week per man as compared with the normal ration of fourteen pounds per week per man given most

---

3.   "The Indians of the North-west," p. 4.

4.   *Ibid.*

5.   "Grievances of the Indians," New York Times, 11 July 1878, p. 5.

6.   The Bannock Indians had tribes living in various areas of the Northwest, some as far south as Wyoming. Ethnically, they are distant relatives of the Sioux and were known for their fierceness as fighters.

3

other tribes at this time.[7] One newspaper article placed the blame

upon the agent, claiming "they [the Bannocks] have been provoked to

hostilities by the lies, frauds, and outrages practiced on them by

their Agent, Reinhart. He made them work, promised them pay, and re-

fused to keep his promises. He starved them, abused them, and lied to

them."[8] But General Crook, after visiting the Indian camp, reported the

agent to be an honest man and cited "insufficient appropriations" as the

reason for a lack of supplies.[9] When the Indian Bureau came under fire

for the lack of funds, the blame was passed to Congress. This appears

to be the true source of the appropriation deficiency, for only four-and-

a-half cents was allocated per Indian per day.[10] Other tribes, such as

the Shoshones, faced similar circumstances which eventually led them to

join the Bannocks when hostilities broke out. General Crook, a defen-

dent of the Indians, after naming "a general complaint of a want of

supplies" as the cause of the war, was asked if it was not hard for the

soldiers to go out and face the threat of death.[11] Keeping in mind the

hunger of the Indians he replied: "That is not the hardest thing. A

harder thing is to be forced to kill the Indians when they are clearly

in the right."[12] Added to their hunger was the Bannocks' distrust of

---

7. "Bannock and Shoshone Indians," New York Times, 29 April 1878, p. 1.

8. "The Provocations to the Indians," New York Times, 29 April 1878, p. 1.

9. "Bannock and Shoshone Indians," p. 1.

10. "Congressional Lapses," New York Times, 25 June 1878, p. 1.

11. "Gen. Crook on the Bannock 'War,'" New York Times, 23 June 1878, p. 5.

12. Ibid.

4

white treaties and policies, such as the agreement signed in 1869.[13]
The combination of all of these "troubles" pushed the Bannock Indians to
war.

   The events which actually precipitated war were the murders of two
white men in August, 1877, and the killing of a man named Alex Rhoden in
November, 1877, by Bannock Indians near Fort Hall, Idaho. The Indian
involved in the first set of murders was handed over to white authorities, but the circumstances surrounding the later murder were not clear.

   Troops, under the command of Colonel John S. Smith, were sent to
Fort Hall to expedite the situation. Smith ordered the Bannocks to
release the Indian accused of murder, but they refused to do so. On
January 9 of the following year, a "heavy military force" surrounded the
Bannock camp on the Snake River and succeeded in forcing the surrender
of the accused murderer. No acts of violence were involved, but weapons
and horses belonging to the Indians were confiscated. This weak sign of
resistance caused many people to suspect an uprising in the spring, as
the Bannocks were considered "well armed, well mounted, and insolent."[14]

   In late May of 1878, "hostilities" began in earnest when two white
settlers were attacked and wounded by a band of Bannock Indians. Soon
after, this group of two hundred warriors made camp near the Camas Prairie in Southern Idaho, and informed the whites that they would be killed
if they did not leave the area. This party was commanded by Buffalo
Horn, a well-known Bannock leader. Ironically, the Indians were supplied

---

   13. In 1869 the Bannocks signed a treaty which gave them the reservation in Southern Idaho. This land was to be for the Bannock tribe
only, but later the Government decided that the various "roaming Indians"
in Idaho should also be placed there. This very much angered the Bannocks.

   14. "Indian Disturbances Apprehended," New York Times, 25 December
1877, p. 1.

5

with weapons and ammunition which they had bought two weeks previously in Boise City, by permission of Governor Braymen who termed them "good Indians." The citizens of Boise denounced Braymen "for his many offenses against the peace and safety of the country" and demanded action.[15] (He was soon replaced by John P. Hoyt as governor of Idaho.) Meanwhile, seventy-five cavalrymen were sent to the area to offer protection to the remaining settlers.

Throughout early June there were scattered reports of raids and murders by the Bannocks. "A serious and extensive outbreak on the part of the redskins, imperiling lives, property, and endangering the mail service [was] anticipated."[16] The Bannocks forced the Shoshone Indians off the Duck Valley Reservation and many of the Shoshones, along with some Weisers and Piutes,[17] joined the "hostiles." A party of Bannocks was reported near Silver City, and soldiers began to escort settlers fleeing to Nevada. The "Indian army" continued to grow and soon numbered about 800 warriors. They attacked trains, stage coaches, and ranches; destroyed stations and houses; and stole cattle. The U.S. Army was able to do little more than watch, while waiting for reinforcements to reach the area.

Both the Indians and army troops began concentrating their forces in mid June. The Bannocks continued to raid ranches and small towns while army reinforcements slowly arrived.[18] During this period of regrouping an interesting episode took place. General Oliver O. Howard

---

15. "The Murdering Indians," New York Times, 9 June 1878, p. 2.

16. "Sitting Bull's Allies," New York Times, 3 June 1878, p. 1.

17. Many of the Piutes were forced to join the Bannocks.

18. In mid June there were rumors of a threatened Indian uprising in Wisconsin. Though never fulfilled, these rumors forced the U.S. Army to keep strong forces in the area, thereby reducing the number of reinforcements sent to Idaho.

6

sent Sarah Winnemucca, daughter of the Piutes' head chief, into the hostile camp to determine whether the Piutes were being held captive or were actually part of the Bannock war party. She disguised herself and sneaked into the camp and returned the night of June 16. She reported that while some Piutes had joined the Bannocks voluntarily, most of them were being held there by force. She also reported that there were Nez Percés in the enemy camp and that Buffalo Horn had been killed, although this last statement proved to be false.[19]

In late June the Indians began to head westward toward Oregon, and were closely pursued by General Howard's troops. Detachments of soldiers took up positions in Idaho and Oregon along the path the "savages" were anticipated to travel. The resulting style of warfare was compared to a "running of the gauntlet" by the Indians through various army units.[20] This "chase" of the hostile Indians by General Howard was to last until the end of the war. On June 23, U.S. troops staged a surprise attack upon the Bannocks on Curry Creek, about 60 miles from Canon City. Under the command of Captain Reuben F. Bernard, the soldiers forced the Indians to fall back into the Stein Mountains, after which they started to move northeastward.[21] A camp "composed of squaws, children, and elderly" was found near the mountains and promptly captured by the troops, who then continued the chase. General Howard praised the soldiers involved as "deserving of high commendation for the gallant and dashing manner in

---

19. Buffalo Horn was killed in a later skirmish.

20. "Close of the Bannock Campaign," Editorial, <u>New York Times</u>, 19 September 1878, p. 4.

21. In some accounts Bernard holds the rank of Captain, in others Major, and in still others Colonel. Since the rank of Captain appears more often in official communiques, it will be presumed to be the proper one.

7

which they inaugurated the campaign."[22]

As the Bannocks and their allies moved through Oregon they were joined by more Indian forces, and Governor Chadwick of Oregon made a call for "arms and men" to protect settlers living in John Day Valley. On July 6, 1878, another engagement took place and the Indians smashed a detachment of volunteers led by Captain Sperry at Willow Springs. After the battle the Indians made for the Columbia River. An advanced group reached the river but were attacked by a gunboat and their camp was demolished. The following day General Howard caught the "renegades" in the Bald Corryel Mountains and dealt them a serious defeat. The Indians scattered into the forests and once again attempted to cross the Columbia River, where they were promptly defeated once more by the gunboat commanded by Captain John A. Kress. The Indians then headed north toward the Umatilla Reservation, in hope of persuading the Umatillas to join them. On July 8, Howard's troops continued the pursuit of the "hostiles."

The Bannocks, having reached the reservation and failing to gain the support of the Umatillas, were attacked at Cayuse Station near Pendleton, Oregon, by units under the command of Captain Evan Miles. The "infamous savages" were soundly beaten once more and fled into the forests and mountains. On July 18, U.S. Cavalry forces, along with some Umatilla Indians, found the enemy camp and easily destroyed it. The "hostiles," finding army troops almost everywhere they turned, began to break into small groups and tried to outrun the ever-pursuing soldiers of General Howard. The Bannocks and Piutes finally separated company, and the small bands of Bannocks headed back toward Idaho. Upon their

---

22. "The Subdued Bannocks," <u>New York Times</u>, 5 November 1878, p. 2.

8

return to Idaho, the Indians staged raids throughout the Camas Prairie, and were then pursued by General Nelson A. Miles' troopers. In early September General Miles engaged the Bannocks moving toward Yellowstone Park at Soda Butte Creek. The Indians fell back to the Park but were attacked again, and after a bitter fight they surrendered. "It was believed that General Miles [had] thus closed the Bannock war."[23]

Upon surrender the Indians were gathered together and held until a decision was reached concerning what was to be done with them. In late November the army received orders to keep the Indian leaders responsible for the war for trial and to escort the remainder to the Simcoe Reservation across the Columbia River. This march took place during the winter, and as a result of improper clothing and food, many of the Indians died along the way. In November, General Miles was accused of acting in a cruel manner to the Indians after they surrendered, but this was disputed by General Sherman.

"Colonel Miles[24] was a good and trusted officer, and had, no doubt, acted properly under the circumstances, well knowing the deceitful character and purposes of these Indians [Bannocks and their Allies], who, after committing all the outrages of which they were capable, proposed to purchase immunity, by a proposition to surrender."[25]

With its deaf ear and insufficient appropriations, the American government and the Indian Department must be held responsible for causing the conflict. The proud Indians, with their natural instinct for survival, cannot and should not be thought of as the guilty party. In

---

23. "Gen. Miles and the Bannocks," New York Times, 14 September 1878, p. 5.

24. General Miles is referred to as a Colonel in some accounts.

25. "The Bannock Indians," New York Times, 6 November 1878, p. 2.

9

fact, it was known in 1878 that Indian uprisings brought troops with fat contracts for local speculators and higher prices for local goods. Many people, such as hog farmers and merchants, were perfectly willing to provoke an uprising for their own material gain. It is customary to suspect dishonesty on the part of the Indian agent, but appropriations were so insufficient that this is highly unlikely. The millions of dollars that were wasted on the transfer of troops, the claims of the various states for services of volunteers, and the damage to private citizens could have been used to prevent the entire incident if the government and military would have possessed the foresight to read the situation properly. Unfortunately, this was not the case and the result is history.

In the end, the "campaign" was only a minor footnote in the history of American Indian warfare. Some people, such as General Crook, sympathized with the Bannocks, but they were a small minority. The general feeling was best exemplified by the words of General Howard: "Success has characterized every movement [of the war], and it is an added source of gratification that all has been accomplished with so small a loss of life on the part of the troops."[26] Unfortunately this attitude prevailed with the general public, with the result that this and other Indian "uprisings" are today looked upon as part of our national shame.

----

26. "The Subdued Bannocks," p. 2.

10

WORKING BIBLIOGRAPHY

"Bannock and Shoshone Indians." New York Times, 29 April 1878, p. 1.

"Bannock Indians, The." New York Times, 6 November 1878, p. 2.

"Brave Indian Squaw, A." New York Times, 17 June 1878, p. 1.

"Close of the Bannock Campaign." Editorial. New York Times, 19 September 1878, p. 4.

"Congressional Lapses." New York Times, 25 June 1878, p. 1.

"Fight on Snake River, Idaho, A." New York Times, 2 August 1878, p. 4.

"Gen. Crook on the Bannock 'War.'" New York Times, 23 June 1878, p. 5.

"Gen. Miles and the Bannocks." New York Times, 14 September 1878, p. 5.

"Gen. Miles Vindicated." New York Times, 11 November 1878, p. 5.

"Grievances of the Indians." New York Times, 11 July 1878, p. 5.

Howard, Oliver O. "Causes of the Piute and Bannock War." Overland Monthly, IX (May 1887), 492-98.

_____. "Results of the Piute and Bannock War." Overland Monthly, XI (February 1888), 192-97.

"Indian Disturbances, The." New York Times, 3 September 1878, p. 1.

"Indian Disturbances Apprehended." New York Times, 25 December 1877, p. 1.

"Indian Massacre Feared, An." New York Times, 19 June 1878, p. 1.

"Indians of the North-west, The." Editorial. New York Times, 12 July 1878, p. 4.

"Indians on the War-Path." New York Times, 7 July 1878, p. 1.

"Marauding Savages, The." New York Times, 21 August 1878, p. 5.

"Movements of Hostile and Friendly Indians--Umatillas Fighting the Snakes." New York Times, 5 July 1878, p. 5.

"Murdering Indians, The." New York Times, 9 June 1878, p. 2.

Miles, General Nelson A. "A Brush With the Bannocks." North American Review, CCCCLXVI (September 1895), 346-51.

11

"Provocations to the Indians, The." New York Times, 1 July 1878, p. 8.

"Restless Savages, The." New York Times, 27 July 1878, p. 5.

"Savages in War Paint, The." New York Times, 30 June 1878, p. 7.

"Scouts Butchered by Indians." New York Times, 2 July 1878, p. 1.

"Sitting Bull's Allies." New York Times, 3 June 1878, p. 1.

"Subdued Bannocks, The." New York Times, 5 November 1878, p. 2.

"Threatened Indian War, The." New York Times, 18 June 1878, p. 1.

"Threatening Indians, The." New York Times, 10 June 1878, p. 1.

"Tribes Further West, The." New York Times, 20 June 1878, p. 5.

"Troublesome Indians, The." New York Times, 21 July 1878, p. 7.

"Trouble with Bannock Indians, The." New York Times, 17 January 1878, p. 1.

"Umatilla and Snake Battle, The." New York Times, 17 July 1878, p. 5.

"Warlike Indians." New York Times, 1 June 1878, p. 1.

"Warlike Indians, The." New York Times, 14 June 1878, p. 1.

"War Painted Savages, The." New York Times, 21 June 1878, p. 1.

THE EXECUTION OF WILLIAM KEMMLER: THE
FIRST MAN TO DIE IN THE ELECTRIC CHAIR

by Barbara Hornbaker

On May 14, 1889, William Kemmler was convicted of murder in the
first degree and sentenced to death, but unlike other convicted murderers who had all gone to the gallows, Kemmler was to be the first criminal "punished by electricity"--a sentence applied in accordance with a
new Code of Criminal Procedure by the State of New York. There was a
great debate about the constitutionality of the law, but after a long
struggle of continuous court appeals, Kemmler was sentenced and resentenced to death in the same manner. Before it ended the controversy
involved the Westinghouse Electric Company and was described by the New
York Times as "an execution that was a disgrace to civilization."

William Kemmler and Tillie Ziegler, a woman who posed as Kemmler's
wife, lived in an apartment in Buffalo, New York. On the night of
March 28, 1889, the drunken Kemmler returned home to find Miss Ziegler
waiting for him in the same condition. The couple had an argument and
Kemmler hit Tillie with the blunt end of a hatchet, killing her instantly. There was a witness who saw the murder, but it did not matter
because Kemmler confessed and stated he was not sorry for what he had
done.[1]

The trial, beginning on August 10, 1889, brought a sentence of
electrocution, and Kemmler was moved to Auburn State Prison to await
execution. Immediately following the trial Mr. Hatch, Kemmler's lawyer,

---

1. "Kemmler Convicted," New York Times, 15 May 1889, p. 3.

1

2

objected to the sentence on the basis that it was cruel and unusual punishment, and therefore unconstitutional. From this plea he apparently received another trial which was the first of three attempts to save Kemmler's life.[2]

Another attempt to save Kemmler's life occurred when a Mr. Cockran took over the case. This was the first hint that interests other than Kemmler's were at stake and at the time these "other interests" were assumed to be the Westinghouse Electric Company.[3] One of the factors that hinted Westinghouse might be involved was that alternating current was to be used in the dynamo that would supply the power in killing Kemmler. At that time people were often electrocuted in the streets from falling cables, and it was assumed that electric companies would not desire the publicity that would result from their type of current being used to execute criminals. Such an insinuation that an electric company might help a murderer escape death aroused the public still further in the case.

A second factor hinting at Westinghouse's involvement was that the dynamo to be used in killing Kemmler was a Westinghouse brand. Again, the company was accused of being involved in the case, and at one point Mr. Westinghouse himself commented: "It is more likely to be those electrical companies who, in the hope of injuring the business of a rival, caused electric-lighting dynamos of a particular manufacture to be adopted by the State for execution purposes."[4]

---

2. This point was never made clear but it is assumed there was another trial immediately following Kemmler's conviction.

3. "Electric Execution of Criminals," Scientific American, 19 October 1889, p. 240.

4. "A Denial from Mr. Westinghouse," New York Times, 4 May 1890, p. 4.

3

When Cockran took over the case in December, 1889, he argued that death would not be instantaneous; therefore, electrical execution was indeed cruel and unusual punishment. Cockran claimed that "a man suffering from electric shock might revive in his coffin . . . and suffer the most exquisite torture."[5] At this point the attorneys consulted experts in electricity to find opinions about whether death would be instantaneous. One of these experts was the renowned Thomas Edison. When questioned, Edison said he felt death would certainly be instantaneous, but that the hands of the victim should be placed in water, since it was such a good conductor of electricity.[6]

Also, in December, 1889, a commission consisting of Dr. Charles MacDonald of the State Lunatic Commission; A. B. Rockwell, an expert on electricity as applied to medicine; Professor Laudy, who was doing research on electrical measurements; and Dr. Fell, one of the first to favor electrocution, was appointed to test the efficiency of the 2000 volt dynamo at Auburn Prison.[7] On December 31, 1889, an old horse and calf were both subjected to an electric current of 1000 volts. They were killed instantly. From this test, as well as others at Sing Sing and Dannemora prisons, the commission concluded the electric chair was truly "efficient."

All the evidence in favor of electrical execution was supposedly collected, but when Kemmler's reprieve was in its last days, a Mr. Sherman mysteriously appeared on the scene with a writ of habeas corpus

---

5. "Electric Execution of Criminals," p. 240.

6. *Ibid*.

7. "Commission Appointed to Test Dynamo," New York Times, 1 January 1890, p. 5.

4

stating the law of electrical execution was unconstitutional under the eighth and fourteenth amendments.[8] Many speculated that Sherman, like Cockran, was a representative of Westinghouse. The acquisition of the writ allowed for an application of error to be filed before the United States Supreme Court, but upon consideration of the application, Chief Justice Fuller announced the Court's refusal to hear the case.[9] Following this setback, Judge Childs, the man who first sentenced Kemmler to die, decreed Kemmler's third and final sentence.

Between the time of the final sentencing and the week of August 4, 1890, the New York Times carried articles describing Kemmler's death chamber and the special chair that had been built. The chamber itself was 17 feet long and 25 feet wide. It was separated into two smaller rooms, one containing the chair itself and the other containing a board mounted with instruments. The only light available to the chamber came from two small grated windows in its roof. The chair had a high back with a headrest with various straps to restrain the head, arms, and legs of the victim. There were also two wires with small electrodes at the ends. The plate which fit over the head of the victim held one of the electrodes, and the other ran down the back of the chair to the base of the victim's spine.

The exact date of the execution was a secret, but as the last days approached Kemmler began to suffer sleepless nights and refused to eat.[10] After listening to the noise of last minute testing, he "cried aloud in

---

8. The eighth amendment prohibits acts of capital punishment that are cruel and unusual. The fourteenth upholds the right to due process.

9. "Kemmler Resentenced," New York Times, 4 July 1890, p. 3.

10. "Kemmler's Last Night," New York Times, 6 August 1890, p. 8.

5

his despair, 'I wish it were over.'"[11] Finally, on the evening of

August 6, Warden Durston visited Kemmler in his cell. Kemmler seemed

very calm and said he wished to "go like a man." In this same conver-

sation he also made the remark to Durston: "I am not afraid so long as

you are in charge of the job. I won't break down if you don't."[12]

On the following morning, Thursday, August 7, 1890, witnesses

began to enter the death cell, with throngs of people around and even

on top of the chamber. One witness was Dr. Fell, who was there to test

his new "resuscitating apparatus" on the body after the electrocution.

At 6:30 a.m. Kemmler was led to the chair and strapped into position.

Then, at 6:43 a.m. the current was applied, and the next events horri-

fied all of the witnesses.

> The body of the man in the chair straightened. Every
> muscle of it seemed to be drawn to its highest tension.
> . . . five seconds passed, ten seconds, fifteen seconds,
> sixteen, and seventeen. Dr. Spitzka, shaking his head,
> said: "He is dead." Warden Durston pressed the signal
> button and at once the dynamo stopped. Then the eyes
> that had been momentarily turned from Kemmler's body
> returned to it and gazed with horror on what they saw.
> The men rose from their chairs impulsively and groaned
> at the agony they felt. "Great God! He is alive!"[13]

It was not known how long the current was on, but when the current was

turned off the body was still heaving. This turn of events forced them

to apply a second electrical shock which produced effects even more

grisly than the first.

> Blood began to appear on the face of the wretch in the
> chair. Sweat stood on the face . . . , but there was worse
> than that. An awful odor began to permeate the death cham-
> ber . . . and it was seen that the hair under and around

_____

11. "Kemmler's Last Night," p. 8.

12. *Ibid*.

13. "Far Worse Than Hanging," New York Times, 7 August 1890, p.12.

6

> the electrode on the head and the flesh . . . around
> the electrode at the base of the spine was singeing.
> The stench was unbearable.[14]

This time the current was on until Kemmler was dead. No one was sure of the amount of the electrical charge applied or of the length of time involved.

Doctors doing the autopsy on Kemmler were so afraid to touch his body immediately after the electrocution that they delayed the autopsy three hours. When the doctors finally did perform the autopsy, there was some disagreement as to whether Kemmler had died after the first shock or had lived and was simply rendered unconscious. There was no doubt he was unconscious after the first shock, but most experts agreed that Kemmler did not die until after the second application of electricity because of the imperfect contact of electrodes.[15] Much of Kemmler's flesh was burned black from the great amount of heat generated and his "inner tissues had been baked."

Various opinions were expressed about the electrocution. One doctor felt that had the current been on for at least thirty seconds the first time, the "experiment" would have been a success. He said that electrocution "is a grand thing, and is destined to become the system of legal death throughout the world."[16] Dr. Spitzka, on the other hand, thought the electrocution was a failure and it impressed him "not exactly with what you would call horror, but rather with wonder and doubt."[17]

---

14. "Far Worse Than Hanging," p. 12.

15. Ibid.

16. Ibid.

17. Ibid.

7

Although this first electrocution was "botched," it was still
maintained as the method for executing criminals in a number of states.
Improvements were made in the apparatus, and since Kemmler's death many
other men and women have died in this manner. One man, a Dr. Shrady,
who witnessed this first electrocution, was prophetic when he declared
"the death chair will yet be the pulpit from which . . . the abolition
of capital punishment will be preached."[18] Today, almost seventy years
after Kemmler's death, capital punishment is still a controversial subject. And whether or not electricity is a proper method is still
undecided; but without question the first execution in this manner was
accurately described by the New York Times as "worthy of the darkest
chambers of the Inquisition of the 16th century."[19]

---

18. "Far Worse Than Hanging," p. 12.

19. Ibid.

8

WORKING BIBLIOGRAPHY

"Another Habeas Corpus Writ." New York Times, 6 May 1890, p. 9.

"Commission Appointed to Test Dynamo." New York Times, 1 January 1890, p. 5.

"Death Is Drawing Nearer." New York Times, 5 August 1890, p. 1.

"Denial from Mr. Westinghouse, A." New York Times, 4 May 1890, p. 4.

"Electric Execution of Criminals." Scientific American, 19 October 1889, p. 240.

"Far Worse Than Hanging." New York Times, 7 August 1890, p. 12.

"Fighting For Kemmler." New York Times, 11 May 1890, p. 8.

"He May Be Killed Today." New York Times, 4 August 1890, p. 1.

"How Will All This End?" New York Times, 1 May 1890, p. 8.

"Kemmler Appeal, The." New York Times, 26 February 1890, p. 6.

"Kemmler Case, The." New York Times, 4 June 1890, p. 3.

"Kemmler Convicted." New York Times, 15 May 1889, p. 3.

"Kemmler Escapes For Awhile." New York Times, 10 June 1890, p. 3.

"Kemmler Finally Sentenced." New York Times, 1 April 1890, p. 3.

"Kemmler Makes His Will." New York Times, 29 April 1890, p. 8.

"Kemmler Resentenced." New York Times, 4 July 1890, p. 3.

"Kemmler Convicted." New York Times, 15 May 1889, p. 3.

"Kemmler's Death Chamber." New York Times, 26 April 1890, p. 2.

"Kemmler's Fate Sealed." New York Times, 25 June 1890, p. 5.

"Kemmler's Fate Undecided." New York Times, 21 May 1890, p. 1.

"Kemmler's Fight For Life." New York Times, 6 May 1890, p. 9.

"Kemmler's Last Night." New York Times, 6 August 1890, p. 8.

"Last Kemmler Decision, The." New York Times, 12 June 1890, p. 3.

9

"Machines That Will Kill." New York Times, 12 February 1890, p. 9.

"No Longer Indifferent." New York Times, 2 August 1890, p. 2.

"Papers in the Case, The." New York Times, 30 April 1890, p. 1.

"Pleading For Kemmler." New York Times, 26 June 1889, p. 3.

"Possible Delay For Kemmler." New York Times, 25 May 1890, p. 1.

"Sherman's Mysterious Client." New York Times, 30 April 1890, p. 1.

"To Die By Electricity." New York Times, 18 May 1889, p. 5.

"To Die By Electricity." New York Times, 22 March 1890, p. 3.

"Trying to Save Kemmler." New York Times, 14 June 1889, p. 1.

THE LAST BARE KNUCKLE PRIZE FIGHT IN AMERICA

by William Calaman

Today, a professional heavyweight fight is viewed as a sophisticated sport and attracts as much publicity and speculation as a presi-
dential election. High-priced announcers devote endless hours of
television time to interviewing the participants, and afterwards the
victor is greeted with wide acclaim--and book contracts. But in the
late 19th century, boxing in America was known as "bare knuckle prize-
fighting," and because of its brutalness, the sport was outlawed in
many states. Fights were conducted in gladiator fashion and matches
continued until one man was beaten into submission and couldn't continue.
Unlike modern boxing, where championship matches consist of fifteen
rounds of three minutes each, rounds in prize-fighting continued until
one fighter was knocked down. In this way it was common for a prize-
fight to last for fifty rounds or more.

Then on July 8, 1889, bare knuckle prize-fighting came to an end in
the swamps of Mississippi with the fight between John L. Sullivan, the
reigning heavyweight champion, and Jake Kilrain. The illegal bout was
staged virtually one step ahead of the law, and within a year after the
bout, both fighters and their associates had been arrested, convicted,
and sentenced for various offences.

The bout was originally scheduled for New Orleans, Louisiana, where
prize fighting was legal, and it was speculated that the champion would
receive the strongest challenge of his career. Not since 1882, when
Sullivan knocked out Paddy Ryan in nine rounds, had the world heavy-

1

2

weight championship changed hands, and so there was a great deal of interest in the contest.[1]

Kilrain, who was training in Baltimore, worked out before "thousands" on any given day, while Sullivan, who was staying in Belfast, New York, had an equally impressive gallery on hand for his daily preparations.[2] On July 6, 1889, both men arrived in New Orleans where they received heroes' welcomes. The betting, it was said, was light, but what little there was favored Sullivan by 2-1 odds.[3]

Meanwhile, the governors of Texas and Mississippi were doing their best to keep the fight from ever materializing. Governor Lowry[4] of Mississippi issued a proclamation on July 1, forbidding the Sullivan-Kilrain fight and offering a $500 reward "for the arrests of principals or participants."[5] Three days later, Governor Ross of Texas, suspicious of a possible fight in Orange County,[6] notified the sheriff there that "Sullivan and Kilrain [may] attempt to come to your county to commit an offense against the public peace of this state. Should they do so, I direct you to use all lawful means to prevent the same."[7]

Governor Lowry went so far as to send the state militia to the

---

1. "Sullivan, John L.," Encyclopedia Britanica, Volume 21, 1970.

2. "Preparing for the Fight," New York Times, 2 July 1889, p. 5.

3. "The Pugilists in New Orleans," New York Times, 7 July 1889, p. 2.

4. The name was spelled in various accounts as "Lowry" or "Lowery."

5. "Sullivan and Kilrain," New York Times, 6 July 1889, p. 2.

6. Orange County is where the Southern Pacific Railroad goes through Texas from New Orleans. In order to transport a large number of people to the fight, the promoters had to be certain that wherever the location was to be, it was near a railroad station.

7. "Sullivan in the South," New York Times, 5 July 1889, p. 2.

3

state line between Mississippi and Louisiana to prevent the fighters
and their parties from crossing into his state. The New York Times
reported on July 6 that "he [Lowry] has directed his sheriffs to watch
all railroads entering the State and spare no expenditure of men and
money to arrest the intruders and prevent the fight."[8]

Governors Lowry and Ross, furthermore, urged their neighbor,
Governor Nicholls of Louisiana, to take comparable measures to keep the
fight out of his state. However, Governor Nicholls was in a bind. He
did not want the fight staged in his state, but at the same time he
feared going against the public which was clamoring for the bout. Perhaps the best indication of public sentiment was revealed when the New
York Times pointed out the fact there was "but one company of sixty-five
men in the militia in New Orleans and its commander, the ever popular
Captain Beanham, is named as a possible referee at the fight."[9] Thus,
the likelihood the fight would occur in New Orleans or a nearby town,
seemed imminent at that point.

The two fighters themselves remained aloof from the legal problems.
After his arrival on Friday, July 5, Sullivan worked out at a local New
Orleans gymnasium.

> "He [Sullivan] arrived under good auspices and in superb
> condition," reported the New York Times. "He has spent
> several hours daily in practice in the gymnasium contig-
> uous to his quarters where he has been crowded by admirers.
> Today he picked up a ten pound solid shot and hurled it
> some twenty feet against a closed door, which was shat-
> tered to splinters."[10]

Kilrain, who was smuggled into New Orleans the follwoing day by the

---

8. "Sullivan and Kilrain," p. 2.

9. Ibid.

10. Ibid.

4

Southern Athletic Club, was busy denying published reports which stated
he had indulged in excessive beer drinking with his friends during a
break in travel at a Chattanooga saloon.[11]

On Sunday, the 7th, the two fighters stayed out of the limelight
that had followed them so carefully the preceeding week. The New York
Times took advantage of the temporary lull in the activity to take its
first editorial stand on the fight. Referring to an incident in New
Orleans during which a large crowd of young boys gathered to give
Sullivan a boisterous welcome, the Times said: "It is such demonstra-
tions as this that emphasize the evils of prize fighting, and make it
imperative that every self-respecting State should stamp out the brutal
practice."[12] The Times further denounced the impending spectacle stating: "It will be a cause of satisfaction to all decent people if the
fight is prevented: it will be still more so if the two principals are
held prisoners in the South until the fight is all taken out of them."[13]

That evening, a special train took Sullivan, Kilrain, their parties, and approximately 2000 fans out of New Orleans towards the
Mississippi line. A surprise proclamation Saturday from Governor
Nicholls, intimating the possibility of using the state militia to prevent the fight and maintain the public peace, had made the excursion
necessary.[14] Although observers did not expect the Louisiana militia
to take action, the entourage made plans to go elsewhere. A request to
move the fight to Arkansas was rejected by Governor Eagle of that

---

11. Ibid.

12. "Editorial," New York Times, 7 July 1889, p. 4.

13. Ibid.

14. "A Fight Certain," The Daily Picayune--New Orleans, 7 July
1889, p. 2.

5

state;[15] however, one of the fight's promoters received an offer from a "prominent Southerner" to have the fight on his property. The anonymous figure, later to be identified as Mr. C. W. Rich of Richburg, Mississippi,[16] also offered "to furnish an indemnity bond and guarantee protection."[17]

Of the train's excursion, the New York Times observed that "at the Mississippi line there was a party of twenty-five men, and the train was challenged, but no attention was paid to the signal, and the special train dashed through at a speed of twenty-five miles an hour. It was just before daybreak when the train got into Mississippi."[18]

At 8 a.m. Monday morning, on the outskirts of Richburg, Mississippi, the fight was scheduled to start. Several items of protocol, such as building a boxing ring, selecting a referee, and giving the local sheriff a chance to stop the fight, delayed the beginning slightly. The referee, by choice of the crowd of some 15,000, was a fellow Southerner, Captain John Fitzgerald.[19] Mr. Corwart, the sheriff of Marion County, stepped into the ring to announce he was commanding peace, but his action was more of a formality than anything else and was virtually meaningless because he had no other officers to back him up. Upon completing his statement, Corwart turned and left the premises, never to return.[20]

---

15. Ibid.

16. "The Bigger Brute Won," New York Times, 9 July 1889, p. 1.

17. "Sullivan's Day," The Daily Picayune--New Orleans, 6 July 1889, p. 2.

18. "The Bigger Brute Won," p. 1.

19. "The Great Battle," The Daily Picayune--New Orleans, 9 July 1889, p. 1.

20. Ibid.

6

From the outset, Sullivan dominated the fight even though Kilrain opened a gash along Sullivan's ear in the seventh round. For the most part Kilrain simply ran around the ring with Sullivan in pursuit. When he was cornered, Kilrain merely fell down, thus ending the round.[21] "This sort of procedure went on for a long time, Kilrain running and dodging and Sullivan calling him to 'fight like a man.'"[22]

In round twenty-three Kilrain shoved a spike from one of his shoes into Sullivan's foot and this caused a near riot among the spectators. In round forty-four Sullivan became ill and fell to one knee but Kilrain was afraid to go near him. He asked him to make the fight a draw, but Sullivan refused, and emphasized the refusal by knocking Kilrain down. He was angry now, and in the next round he not only knocked Kilrain down, but he jumped on him, which prompted a claim of foul from Kilrain's friends. This was not allowed, and it was repeated in the next round, after Sullivan again threw Kilrain and fell on him.[23]

At round seventy-five the referee cautioned Kilrain that if he continued to fall down without being hit he would disqualify him. Realizing his fighter was beaten, Kilrain's second threw a sponge in the ring to indicate the fight was over.

> When Donovan threw up the sponge for Kilrain there was
> a wild confusion and a general rush for the ring was made.
> The reporters' desks were splintered, fences went down,
> and all restrictions were swept aside. An exit for Sul-
> livan was cleared by Muldoon [his trainer] and Cleary by
> vigorous movements of the arms. The victor was placed in
> a carriage and conveyed to the train.[24]

---

21. "The Great Battle," p. 1.

22. *Ibid.*

23. "The Bigger Brute Won," p. 1.

24. *Ibid.*

7

After the fight, Kilrain was quoted as saying, "I couldn't do my best; that is what makes me feel so mean. . . . I ran around. I did it for my friends. I was not strong at the start."[25] Kilrain's comments were ironic in that he had spent the entire week before the fight denying reports that he was "tired" and not in top form.[26]

On the following day, the attention of the public went from fight to flight. In the same edition in which the New York Times reported the results of the bout, there was an editorial recommending that participants in and backers of the fight be punished.

On Thursday, July 11, Sullivan was arrested in Nashville, Tennessee, but was released that same afternoon after his attorneys attained a writ of habeas corpus. An eager Governor Lowry, immediately after hearing of the arrest, issued a statement offering $500 for the arrest of Jake Kilrain so the two could be tried together. Sullivan, however, left that evening to escape further north to Chicago. Realizing that authorities meant business and were not just trying to put up a front, Sullivan's backers jumped off the train three blocks from the main terminal in Chicago, where authorities were once again waiting.

Even with his brush with the law, Sullivan did not fear capture, let alone a jail sentence. He confidently went where he wanted to and drank himself into a stupor whenever he felt like it while he was in Chicago. Kilrain was also sure that the most that would happen would be a fine; however his trainer, Charlie Mitchell, did not share Kilrain's confidence. Mitchell, disguised as an Indian, fled to Wisconsin and then, to throw off his pursuers, he doubled back and spent two nights

---

25. Ibid.

26. "Sullivan in the South," p. 2.

8

sleeping in the cornfields of Indiana. He then put on a priest's garb
and made it to Buffalo, New York. From there he booked passage to
England.[27]

Sullivan and Kilrain enjoyed a brief hiatus for several weeks
after the fight, but the honeymoon ended on August 1 when Sullivan was
apprehended in New York after Governor Lowry issued still another request for the arrest of the fighters.[28] Sullivan offered no resistance,
and readily agreed to go to Pervis, Mississippi, for the trial, if one
was deemed necessary.[29] Apparently more concerned with his image than
with his arrest, Sullivan issued the following statement:

> I have nothing to say about my recent victory. What I
> do want you to say is that you saw me sober. I have been
> sober ever since I left New Orleans. I have been keeping
> quiet in a friend's house in Chicago. I know that in the
> past I have done much that deserves the condemnation it
> received, but what has been said regarding my drinking and
> carousing since the fight is false. Tomorrow I am going
> to Boston to spend a week with my mother. . . .[30]

Sullivan's attorney, Mr. DeLancy Nicoll, pleaded in the preliminary
trial in New York[31] that Sullivan had no intention of fighting in Mississippi, but that the location was changed at the last minute and Sullivan did not know where the train was taking him.[32] Afterwards, Sullivan was to be taken to Pervis for trial on Monday, August 12, but in

---

27. "Mitchell Arrives in England," New York Times, 29 July 1889,
p. 1.

28. "Sullivan Arrested," New York Times, 1 August 1889, p. 1.

29. Ibid.

30. "Sullivan Says He Was Sober," New York Times, 1 August 1889,
p. 2.

31. There had to first be a hearing to determine whether Sullivan
should be sent to Mississippi to stand trial.

32. "Sullivan Goes South," New York Times, 2 August 1889, p. 8.

9

keeping with the aura of the times, a bookmaker from New Orleans offered
to pay $500 of any fine Sullivan and Kilrain might have assessed against
them in exchange for an exhibition match.[33]

In early August, Sullivan left Grand Central train station for
Mississippi "amidst the cheers of a delirious crowd." When he arrived
in Jackson, Mississippi, Sullivan registered at the local hotel and had
dinner sent to his room. (Governor Lowry, upon hearing this, demanded
that Sullivan be put in jail.)

At the trial Sullivan's defense was that it was all a case of mis-
taken identity, that he was not the same man who had been involved in
the fight. However, on the witness stand, he pleaded for understanding
and asked the jammed courtroom: "What's a feller goin' to do when he
can't follow his business! Fightin' is my business. That's how I make
a livin' and I ain't got no other way of doin' it."[34]

By the time August 12 rolled around, most observers expected the
Sullivan trial to end in some kind of compromise, but on August 16
District Attorney Neville gave his closing argument and demanded that:

> From the evidence the accused has been proved guilty.
> If your verdict be that he is not guilty, then write
> the indictment: "Not guilty. Mississippi disgraced
> and despised." And if the verdict be "Guilty," then
> you will show the world that in Mississippi, our be-
> loved State, the law is supreme.[35]

Apparently this argument (and the evidence) was effective, and to
the astonishment of many, Sullivan was convicted. "He tried to keep up
his spirits, singing a snatch of song and forcing a laugh, but he was

---

33. "Kilrain Arrested," New York Times, 6 August 1889, p. 1.

34. "The Bruiser's Trial," New York Times, 13 August 1889, p. 1.

35. "Sullivan Convicted," New York Times, 17 August 1889, p. 1.

10

evidently a little downhearted."[36]

The following day Sullivan was sentenced to one year in prison. "A prediction two months ago," the *Times* wrote, "that Sullivan would spend a year in the Marion County Jail would have been laughed at. Today his friends are terribly anxious about the outlook, although they still strain their eyes for a glimpse of an opening in the clouds which now hang over him so steadily."[37]

Meanwhile, Kilrain was out on bail in Baltimore, awaiting his trial which would begin on August 22. It was reported that he was "greatly depressed"[38] when he heard of Sullivan's sentence, but when his case finally came up he was given a mere two months sentence. Ironically, Kilrain was not found guilty of prize fighting, as Sullivan was, but rather of assault and battery.[39]

On March 17, 1890, the Supreme Court ruled that the indictment against Sullivan was "fatally defective" and Sullivan was set free. Within a week of the court's decision on the Sullivan matter, Kilrain was set 'free' because his friend, Charlie W. Rich, was given legal custody of him for the length of his two month sentence.[40] The *Times* did not elaborate on the arrangement except to say that Mr. Rich delivered a check for "an undisclosed amount" to the Marion County Commissioners.[41]

Sullivan returned to the ring, and successfully defended his title,

---

36. *Ibid.*

37. "Jail for Sullivan," *New York Times*, 18 August 1889, p. 1.

38. *Ibid.*

39. "Kilrain Convicted," *New York Times*, 15 December 1889, p. 1.

40. "Kilrain Released," *New York Times*, 25 March 1890, p. 1.

41. *Ibid.*

11

with gloves, until 1892, when he was knocked out by James J. Corbett in 21 rounds in New Orleans.[42] After retiring from the ring, Sullivan became involved in the cause of prohibition, and spent the rest of his life traveling around the country giving speeches on the evils of alcohol. He died in modest circumstances in 1918. Kilrain continued fighting, but never again came close to claiming a world championship. He faded into obscurity, and reportedly died in the early 1900s.

And so ended America's last bare-knuckle prize fight as participants were then required to wear gloves and the sport faded from the public eye for a few years. Today, one looks back nostagically at the era, with the yellowed pictures of mustachioed strong men striking a fighter's pose, and little realize how brutal the contests really were. Still, with the passing of any era, there are those men who are trapped in time and unable to bridge the gap. It would seem that John L. Sullivan may have been such a person, and this author is struck with the man's plea at his trial: "What's a feller goin' to do when he can't follow his business!" It is a lament one hears as clearly today as in 1889 from people in all walks of life who find their livelihood has become obsolete.

---

42. "Sullivan, John L." <u>Encyclopedia Britanica</u>, Volume 21, 1970.

12

WORKING BIBLIOGRAPHY

"Big Brute Arrested, The." New York Times, 12 July 1889, p. 1.

"Bigger Brute Won, The." New York Times, 9 July 1889, p. 1.

"Bruisers at the Ring." New York Times, 8 July 1889, p. 5.

"Bruiser's Trial, The." New York Times, 13 August 1889, p. 1.

"Bruisers Working South." New York Times, 4 July 1889, p. 5.

"Editorial." New York Times, 7 July 1889, p. 4.

"Fight Certain, A." The Daily Picayune--New Orleans, 7 July 1889, p. 2.

"Great Battle, The." The Daily Picayune--New Orleans, 9 July 1889, p. 1.

"Jail for Sullivan." New York Times, 18 August 1889, p. 1.

"Kilrain Arrested." New York Times, 6 August 1889, p. 1.

"Kilrain Before the Court." New York Times, 15 December 1889, p. 1.

"Kilrain Convicted." New York Times, 15 December 1889, p. 1.

"Kilrain Must Stand Trial." New York Times, 23 August 1889, p. 2.

"Kilrain Released." New York Times, 25 March 1890, p. 5.

"Looking For the Bruisers." New York Times, 10 July 1889, p. 1.

"Mitchell Arrives in England." New York Times, 29 July 1889, p. 1.

"Preparing For the Fight." New York Times, 2 July 1889, p. 5.

"Prize Fight." Editorial. New York Times, 9 July 1889, p. 4.

"Pugilist Arrested in Tennessee." Editorial. New York Times, 12 July 1889, p. 4.

"Pugilists in New Orleans, The." New York Times, 7 July 1889, p. 2.

"Pursuing the Pugilists." New York Times, 16 July 1889, p. 1.

"Slugger Sullivan in Jail." New York Times, 5 August 1889, p. 1.

"Sullivan and his Friends." New York Times, 3 August 1889, p. 1.

"Sullivan and Kilrain." New York Times, 6 July 1889, p. 2.

13

"Sullivan Arrested." New York Times, 1 August 1889, p. 1.

"Sullivan Arrives in New Orleans." Editorial. New York Times, 7 July
     1889, p. 4.

"Sullivan Convicted." New York Times, 17 August 1889, p. 1.

"Sullivan's Day." The Daily Picayune--New Orleans, 6 July 1889, p. 2.

"Sullivan Goes South." New York Times, 2 August 1889, p. 8.

"Sullivan Indictment Quashed." New York Times, 18 March 1890, p. 1.

"Sullivan, John L." Encyclopedia Britanica, Volume 21, 1970.

"Sullivan in Mississippi." New York Times, 7 August 1889, p. 1.

"Sullivan in the South." New York Times, 5 July 1889, p. 2.

"Sullivan Says He Was Sober." New York Times, 1 August 1889, p. 2.

REVEREND HANS SCHMIDT: PHYSICIAN, PRIEST, MURDERER

by Linda Trznadel

On September 6, 1913, two children spotted a large brown bundle floating down the Hudson River near the New Jersey shore. The older boy recovered the package and took it home to his mother who slowly began to unwrap the parcel in front of some neighborhood children. Inside the bundle was a flowered pillow, and inside the pillow, among the feathers, was the upper torso of a woman's body--"the head and arms neatly removed."[1]

The torso was taken to the morgue where the county physician, George King, stated that "the dismemberment was done skillfully and might be the work of a surgeon. The flesh has been cut clean with a sharp knife and the bones . . . cut with a surgical saw."[2] It was further determined she was a little over 20 years old and had been dead about three or four days.

The following day the lower part of the body was found floating in the river about three miles below the point where the first part was discovered. Again the body was found in a pillow case half filled with feathers, but this time it was packed with a rock identified as "schist," a type of stone abundant in Manhattan but seldom found in New Jersey. An examination showed the "woman died undergoing an operation because the two pieces fit perfectly. The legs were severed two inches below

---

1. "Find Woman's Body in Bundle in River," New York Times, 7 September 1913, p. 3.

2. Ibid.

1

2

the hip, evidently done by a surgeon's saw."[3] The autopsy showed the murder was more brutal than first suspected and it was believed the victim was tortured before her death. The coroner stated that the limbs could have been amputated while the woman was still alive. Also, it was determined that shortly before death the woman had had a premature child.[4]

The task of piecing together the details of the crime fell to Inspector Faurot, a veteran New York Police officer. Although there was little to go on he did have one substantial clue. The second part of the body was wrapped similarly to the first, but this time a pillow case rather than another pillow was used. On this pillow slip was embroidered the letter "A" with fancy designs on either side and it also bore a tag with the name of the Robinson-Rodgers Company of Newark. Inspector Faurot contacted the company manager for help and learned the pillow case was one of a group sold to the Sack's Furniture Store in New York. A check of the store's books showed pillow cases of the same size and design had been delivered to 68 Bradhurst Street, an apartment building in New York. The purchaser of the pillow case as well as other merchandise was recorded as a "Reverend Hans Schmidt."

Schmidt's apartment was put under surveillance, but after watching the apartment for several days police became suspicious and decided to break in and conduct an investigation. After searching the room, it became evident that the murder had been committed there.

There was a dark stain on the green wallpaper, another stain on the floor in the hall between the bedroom and bathroom, and a new scrub

---

3. "River Yields More of Woman's Body," New York Times, 8 September 1913, p. 3.

4. Police did not think this fact was connected with her death.

3

brush was on the sink along with six cakes of soap. The white enamel bed contained bed springs, but the mattress, bedding and pillow had been removed. There were two trunks in the room, a steamer trunk and a small zinc trunk which contained a package of 50 or 60 letters sent to an "Anna Aumuller" from various addresses. When detectives opened the larger trunk they found a bunch of women's clothes, a butcher knife 15 inches long, and a large hand saw. The knife had been sharpened on a stone and both had been scoured. Most of the letters proved of little help, but several mentioned the rectory of St. Boniface as the place where the girl worked.

After questioning the pastor of the Church, Reverend J. S. Brown, Inspector Faurot learned that Anna Aumuller had worked there as a servant and also that the Reverend Hans Schmidt had been connected with the church at the same time. The Inspector was also told that Reverend Hans Schmidt was now preaching at St. Joseph's Church and so Faurot closed the interview and immediately proceeded to St. Joseph's Church. Upon first meeting Reverend Hans Schmidt, Inspector Faurot became very suspicious since the man appeared quite nervous. When Faurot questioned him about knowing the murdered girl, Schmidt denied knowing her several times. Finally the Inspector pulled out a picture of the girl and showed it to the priest. Schmidt still insisted he did not know her, but Inspector Faurot continued his questioning while the priest became more and more nervous.

When he saw how much the detectives actually knew, "he sank into a chair and began to weep." "Yes, I killed her," said Schmidt as he finished crying. "I killed her because I loved her, I am guilty and I

4

am ready to pay the penalty."[5]

Schmidt then began to relate the circumstances surrounding his relationship with Anna Aumuller. He claimed he had been ordained a priest in Mainz, Germany, in 1904 and in 1909 came to America and served as an assistant to Father Braun, the rector at St. Boniface's Church. Here he met Anna Aumuller. Schmidt admitted having relations with the girl while he was a priest at St. Boniface's. He explained he obtained a marriage license and performed the ceremony himself. In November 1912, he left St. Boniface and became assistant pastor to the Reverend Gerard H. Huntihamm, rector of St. Joseph's Church, but he still continued to live with Anna in the apartment at 68 Bradhurst Avenue. Finally, he decided he must kill his "wife," because if detected he would be excommunicated from the Church.

Schmidt confessed that on September 2, 1913, he entered the apartment where Anna Aumuller was sleeping and slit the woman's throat. He then carried the body into the bathroom, placed it in the bathtub, and proceeded to dismember the body with a butcher knife and a saw. Through the night and early into the morning, Schmidt said he made several trips to the river with packages containing parts of the body. Some of the pieces were weighed with schist and were wrapped in the blankets, sheets, pillow and pillowslip that were on the bed. After the mattress was destroyed by fire, Schmidt stated he scrubbed the floors of the apartment to remove traces of the blood. He removed things from the apartment in the days following the crime, but after the first section of the body was discovered, he said he never returned. When asked about the dissection Schmidt replied: "I studied surgery for several months in

---

5. "River Murder Traced to Priest Who Confesses Today," <u>New York Times</u>, 15 September 1913, p. 1.

5

Germany." In support of his other career Schmidt produced a business
card inscribed: "Dr. Emil Moliere, formerly assistant surgeon of the
Municipal Woman's Hospital, Paris, France, Representative of the
Chemical Hygiene Manufacturing Company."[6]

This fact revealed a new aspect to the murder case. It was now
discovered that Schmidt was in partnership with a Dr. Ernest Arthur
Muret, a man who practiced dentistry under false credentials. Together
they conducted illegal operations, printed their own birth and death
certificates, and counterfeited money. When Dr. Muret was arrested he
confessed to the charge of counterfeiting and a search of his office
uncovered presses, chemicals, and photographic plates. Inspector Faurot
was amazed at what was uncovered and exclaimed:

> I have seen crazy men who have tried to make counter-
> feits with a pen and ink and a poor set of tools, but I
> have never known one with the brains to fit up a plant
> that could turn out such high quality imitation money.
> . . .[7]

When Schmidt was asked of the counterfeiting, he said he was going
to use the money for "social purposes." He replied: "There are so many
poor and miserable people in the world it would be better if fewer were
born. My mission was to prevent children from being born to a life of
misery." He went further in justifying his ideas by saying, "I am a
believer in euthanasia. I believe that the crippled, the diseased, and
all who are suffering beyond remedy from physical or mental troubles
should be put to a painless death."[8] Schmidt said he planned to murder

---

6. "River Murder Traced to Priest," p. 1.

7. "Schmidt and Muret Indicted as Coiners," New York Times, 24
September 1913, p. 2.

8. "Schmidt Brought Women to America," New York Times, 21 September 1913, p. 2.

6

the victims and then fill out the death certificates to make it appear

as though the victims died a natural death.[9]

When Father Luke J. Evers, the Chaplain at the Tombs,[10] visited

Schmidt and questioned him about his reasons for killing Anna Aumuller,

Schmidt responded: "I was in love with the girl, and I wanted her to

go to heaven. It was necessary to make a sacrifice, and the sacrifice

had to be consummated in blood in the same manner as Abraham was going

to sacrifice Isaac."[11] When asked why he disposed of the body in the

river, Schmidt explained the sacrifice must be consummated in blood and

water so the fragments could go into "clouds of eternity." At this

point an all-out effort was made by the Catholic Church to prove that

Schmidt had never been ordained as a priest and had used false creden-

tials to obtain positions in various churches.[12]

At Schmidt's trial his lawyer entered a plea of guilty but argued

the Priest was insane at the time of the crime. Alienists[13] for the

defense testified on a family history of insanity and Schmidt's father

was brought over from Germany to testify to his son's unusual childhood

behavior. District Attorney Delehanty tried to disprove Schmidt's

assertion that "the Deity commanded him to commit the murder." He

showed that in April, 1913, Schmidt tried to secure an insurance policy

---

9. "Chain of Murders Schmidt's Plan," New York Times, 20 September
1913, p. 1.

10. The Tombs was the name for the New York City detention center.

11. "River Murder Traced to Priest," p. 1.

12. Father Evers asked Schmidt who ordained him and Schmidt replied:
"St. Elizabeth, Patron Saint of Hungary." Although church authorities
presented records to show Schmidt was never a priest, this writer is
unconvinced.

13. Psychiatrists.

7

for $5,000 on Anna Aumuller's life and named himself beneficiary of the policy.[14] With this evidence Schmidt was found guilty of murder in the first degree by a unanimous vote of the jury. He greeted the verdict with a laugh and said he wanted to die immediately.

Even though Schmidt was found guilty, his lawyer said he would try to get an appeal. He argued that Schmidt did not kill Anna, but he confessed to the murder to cover for someone else. He argued that Anna died of an operation and Schmidt dismembered her body to dispose of it more easily.[15] The first appeal was refused however, and Justice M. Davis sentenced Schmidt to die in the electric chair during the week of March 23, 1914. Still, it was close to two years later before Hans Schmidt was executed. Further charges of counterfeiting were leveled against the former priest and extended court appeals delayed the inevitable.[16] Eventually, on February 12, 1916, Hans Schmidt was taken to Sing Sing to await execution. He refused to see reporters, but sent them the following brief poem:

> Beyond this vale of tears
>   There is life above,
> Unmeasured by the flight of years,
>   And all that life, is love.[17]

---

14. "Schmidt Purposed to Kill for Money," New York Times, 23 September 1913, p. 5.

15. A year later Schmidt wrote a letter to Assistant District Attorney Delehanty stating he "induced Dr. Muret to perform an operation on Anna from the effects of which she died." "Hans Schmidt Confesses," New York Times, 13 December 1914, p. 12.

16. At the same time Anna Aumuller was not buried until August 24, 1915, after being in the "icebox" at the morgue for two years. Authorities explained that the body was not buried sooner because the head had not been found. "Schmidt's Victim to Potters Field," New York Times, 25 August 1915, p. 7.

17. "Schmidt in Sing Sing," New York Times, 12 February 1916, p. 18.

8

Six days later he was strapped in the electric chair. "My last word is
to say good-bye to my dear old mother," he concluded. A signal was
given and after three shocks the Reverend Hans Schmidt was pronounced
dead.

An evaluation of this case leads one to suspect that not every
facet of the crime came out at the trial. Indeed, the role of Dr. Muret
is puzzling and one is inclined to believe he was an accomplice in
Anna's death. Schmidt's death house assertion that she died of a
botched abortion makes sense when it is remembered that the autopsy
showed the girl had recently given birth to a premature child. And
when Muret's office was searched, a number of obstetrical instruments
and books on gynecology were found. Thus, it seems logical to assume
that Schmidt, upon being told of Anna's pregnancy, convinced the servant
girl to undergo an abortion--an operation which Muret had apparently
performed on previous young ladies. When she accidentally died, Schmidt
then panicked and disposed of the corpse. Police seemed to show little
interest in prosecuting Muret beyond one count of counterfeiting (he
was sentenced to seven years on this charge), and Schmidt was left trying to defend himself against the claim that he had dismembered the
girl while she was still alive. In Schmidt's confession on the day of
his execution he stated, "that I am going to my death not for murder,
but for lying. Anna Aumuller really died from the results of an operation for which I was morally responsible, and being morally responsible
I lied in my defense of insanity in order that I might not drag those
to ruin who took part in the operation."[18] One is inclined to believe
this explanation and conclude that convicting Schmidt of first degree

18. "Hans Schmidt Dies Today," New York Times, 18 February 1916,
p. 12.

9

murder--while not even indicting Muret--was a miscarriage of justice. In conclusion it would seem that placing complete blame for murder on Schmidt alone was far too severe.

10

WORKING BIBLIOGRAPHY

"Arrest Dentist as Schmidt's Aid in Coining Plant." New York Times, 16
    September 1913, p. 1.

"Chain of Murders Schmidt's Plan." New York Times, 20 September 1913,
    p. 2.

"Find Woman's Body in Bundle in River." New York Times, 7 September
    1913, p. 11.

"Girl Cast into River; Murdered Says Physician." Philadelphia Inquirer,
    7 September 1913, p. 8.

"Hans Schmidt Confesses." New York Times, 13 December 1914, p. 12.

"Hans Schmidt Dies Today." New York Times, 18 February 1916, p. 12.

"Muret Denies Plan to Accuse Schmidt." New York Times, 27 September
    1913, p. 9.

"Nearer to Solving River Murder." New York Times, 10 September 1913,
    p. 3.

"Priest is Shamming Dr. MacDonald Says." New York Times, 27 December
    1913, p. 6.

"River Murder Traced to Priest Who Confesses." New York Times, 15
    September 1913, p. 1.

"River Yields More of Woman's Body." New York Times, 8 September 1913,
    p. 2.

"Schmidt and Muret Indicted as Coiners." New York Times, 24 September
    1913, p. 20.

"Schmidt Brought Women to America." New York Times, 21 September 1913,
    p. 2.

"Schmidt to Be Executed for Slaying Girl." New York Times, 2 February
    1916, p. 12.

"Schmidt in Sing Sing." New York Times, 12 February 1916, p. 18.

"Schmidt is Guilty in the First Degree." New York Times, 6 February
    1914, p. 1.

Schmidt Jury Not Agreed; Locked Up." New York Times, 30 December 1913,
    p. 1.

11

"Schmidt Must Die; Loses Final Appeal." New York Times, 8 January
      1916, p. 5.

"Schmidt Purposed to Kill for Money." New York Times, 23 September
      1913, p. 5.

"Schmidt Ready for More Death." New York Times, 19 September 1913, p. 1.

"Schmidt Seeks Clemency." New York Times, 25 April 1914, p. 10.

"Schmidt's Victim to Potters Field." New York Times, 25 August 1915, p. 7.

"Sends Muret to Prison." New York Times, 29 October 1913, p. 20.

"Still Fight For Schmidt." New York Times, 7 February 1914, p. 3.

"Trace River Victim by Sale of Pillows." New York Times, 9 September
      1913, p. 2.

"U.S. Agents Search Schmidt Evidence." New York Times, 17 September
      1913, p. 1.

GRACE HUMISTON, THE FIRST WOMAN DETECTIVE

by Tim McCarl

On July 18, 1948, a small article appeared in the New York Times
entitled, "Mrs. Humiston, 77, Crime Lawyer, Dies." The paper, in a few
short paragraphs, summarized the life and career of Mrs. Mary Grace
Humiston, crusading lawyer and sleuth extraordinary. The lady, like her
obituary, has long since been forgotten, but at the height of her career
during World War I she was one of the most respected and influential
women in the city of New York and perhaps in the entire state. For at
a time in our nation's history when everyone had more than their share
of troubles, Grace Humiston dedicated herself to the cause of others
who needed her help desperately. Her prowess as a detective was so
highly regarded that one reporter referred to her as "Mrs. Sherlock
Holmes." Bewildered, frightened underdogs were her clients and justice
was her guiding light. However, she was also an ardent crusader who
worked feverishly to wipe out vice and corruption, even to the point of
sacrificing her own career. As her life story reveals, she should be
remembered as Mrs. Humiston the woman, as well as the detective, for she
dedicated herself to fighting for the improvement of conditions which
were prevalent in her day and ours.

Born in Greenwich Village, New York City, in 1871, Mary Grace
Winterton was the daughter of Mr. and Mrs. Adoniram Judson Winterton.
Mr. Winterton was a well-to-do merchant who engrained into his daughter
the extreme upright morality of the Baptist faith. Following her gradu-
ation from Hunter College in 1888, Grace Winterton taught for several

1

2

years at a school in New York City. Dissatisfied with the teaching profession she attended classes at the New York Evening Law School, where she graduated seventh in her class in 1904. For a while she worked as a clerk in the Legal Aid Society, but upon entering the bar in 1905 she was instrumental in founding a law office known as the People's Law Firm, which was intended for the less wealthy clients.

From the very beginning the People's Law Firm received many reports of missing persons who were discovered to be working in lumber camps in the South which produced raw turpentine. Suspecting some sort of enslavement of workers, Miss Winterton was anxious to investigate these Southern lumber camps. During 1906 and 1907 she disguised herself and observed many of the camps close up. She discovered these camps recruited unemployed men from big cities in the North to work in the camps. Once down South, however, the volunteer workers were virtually made slaves and not permitted to return home. Her findings led to an exposé of these conditions and resulted in the outlaw of such practices.

Not long after this, Grace Winterton toured several foreign countries while investigating the activities of steamship companies which lured peasants to America in an attempt to gain their ship fares. During a stay in Lima, Peru, she married Howard Humiston, one of her colleagues in the People's Law Firm. Once back in the United States the Humistons settled down to housekeeping, but Mrs. Humiston was soon deeply involved in her work. She accepted the case of Gennaro Mazella,[1] sentenced to die in Sing Sing Prison in August, 1915, for the murder of a girl named Andrea Castiglano.[2] An acquittal was finally gained by Mrs. Humiston

---

1. Also referred to as Gennaro Mazzella.

2. "Two Sentenced to Die," *New York Times*, 29 June 1915, p. 9.

3

from the New York Supreme Court which saved Mazella from the death penalty.[3]

As Mrs. Humiston's fame as a lawyer grew, it attracted the attention of many people throughout New York state. One such person was Spencer Miller, Deputy Warden of Sing Sing. Miller felt she was the only one who could prove the innocence of convict Charles F. Stielow, an illiterate farmer condemned to die in the electric chair for a double murder. Following a meeting with Miller on July 4, 1915, Mrs. Humiston came to agree with Miller on the innocence of Stielow and immediately set about to clear him.

Stielow had worked for a wealthy farmer named Charles B. Phelps of West Shelby, Orleans County, in the western part of the state. On the night of March 21, Phelps was shot to death in the kitchen of his home during an apparent robbery of his house. Miss Margaret Wolcott, Phelps' housekeeper, was found dead the next morning on the doorstep of Charles Stielow's house, which was directly across the road from Phelps' home.[4] Police began to search the county for the murderer after being summoned to the scene of the crime, but not until two weeks later were Stielow and his brother-in-law Nelson Green[5] taken into custody. The two confessed they had killed Phelps and his housekeeper when they attempted to rob the man.[6] On the basis of these confessions the two men were tried

---

3. Only one short article on the case was found.

4. "Confess Double Murder," New York Times, 24 April 1915, p. 7.

5. Some articles listed Green as Stielow's nephew.

6. The written confession obtained by the detectives in charge was not signed. Stielow later told Deputy Warden Miller he was innocent and had agreed to the confession only in order to end a third degree interrogation he endured for two days.

4

for murder and Stielow was condemned to death while Green got life imprisonment.

Due to an examination by a psychiatrist which revealed Charles Stielow possessed the mind of a seven-year-old, Mrs. Humiston was convinced of the worthlessness of the confession.[7] Although the case dragged on into 1916 she never gave up hope and constantly fought for reprieves of Stielow's death sentence while searching for the real killer.[8] These reprieves gave her time to investigate a report of a visit by a peddler to the Phelps house on the night of the murder, whom she suspected to be Orleans County junk dealer Irving King.[9] In the presence of Mrs. Humiston, police detectives, and legal officials, King admitted he and Clarence O'Connell, an Auburn Prison convict, were responsible for the murders of Charles Phelps and Margaret Wolcott.

Although the two were arrested for the double homicide, many still were unconvinced of the guilt of King and O'Connell. Several days after making his confession, King denied the charges and stated he had been offered $3000 and an eventual pardon by Governor Whitman to take the blame.[10] The two were again incriminated, though, by the testimony of Charles and Laura Laskey, O'Connell's landlords at the time of the murders. They stated O'Connell had been out with a buggy on the night of March 21 and later had shot his horse with a bullet which matched the

---

7. The psychiatrist determined the accused man had a vocabulary of only 150 words. However, the confession contained over 350 words.

8. One such reprieve came on July 29, 1916, less than an hour before Stielow was to be executed, when Mrs. Humiston provided State Supreme Court Justice Charles L. Guy with evidence of the identity of the true killer.

9. Appears also as Erwin King.

10. "King Now Retracts Murder Confession," New York Times, 15 August 1916, p. 5.

5

two .22 caliber slugs found in Charles Phelps' body.[11] A Grand Jury
trial in December of 1917 failed to indict Irving King and Clarence
O'Connell of murder and nothing definite was decided.[12]

Governor Whitman had commuted Stielow's death sentence to life
imprisonment in late 1916. With an undecisive verdict the only result
of the 1917 Grand Jury investigation of the Stielow case, the Governor
was urged by members of the Jury to drop charges against Stielow and
Green. Finally, on May 9, 1918, Whitman exonerated Charles F. Stielow
and Nelson Green of all charges. The next day Charles Stielow, after
three agonizing years in prison and seven last minute reprieves from
the electric chair, left Sing Sing and tried to salvage his life. His
story remains an unfortunate example of the shortcomings of the American
legal system.

Throughout the long period Stielow was awaiting an acquittal, Mrs.
Humiston became engaged in another case which, like the Stielow case,
was to be one of her most important. Seventeen-year-old Ruth Cruger had
gone to pick up her ice skates which were being sharpened at a nearby
shop in New York City on February 13, 1917. By 7 p.m. Ruth had not returned and her older sister Helen phoned the authorities.[13] Police
searched the motorcycle shop of Alfredo Cocchi where the Cruger girl was
said to have taken her skates, but she was not there. They ascertained
she had picked up the skates and left the shop. Meanwhile, Henry Cruger

---

11. "Open New Fight to Save Stielow," New York Times, 28 September
1916, p. 7.

12. Further research failed to reveal whether or not the two were
ever found guilty. The last reference to them after the trial stated
O'Connell was still in Auburn Prison for shooting a man and King had
disappeared.

13. The girl's father, Henry D. Cruger, a public accountant, was
in Boston on business at the time.

6

had hired several private detectives in an effort to locate his missing daughter.

Three days after the disappearance of the girl Mrs. Alfredo Cocchi reported her husband was also missing. He had closed his shop early on the afternoon of the 13th and didn't come home until 10:00 p.m. The next morning he borrowed five dollars from his wife and she hadn't seen him since. There accompanied Mrs. Cocchi's statement literally hundreds of reports by people claiming to have seen girls fitting Ruth Cruger's description over the preceeding few weeks. Several stories were received that a girl and a man had entered a taxicab together near Cocchi's around 3:00 o'clock on the day of the disappearance. Henry Cruger became infuriated by a theory of the police suggesting his daughter eloped and he still maintained she was kidnapped.

During the following month Mrs. Humiston read about the case with mild interest. She agreed to make an investigation for the Cruger family only when she was urged to do so in April by Mrs. Felix Adler, a rich New York socialite. Like Mr. Cruger, she dismissed the police's idea of elopement. But, as she later told reporters, "I somehow felt . . . Ruth had been murdered . . . therefore, I went to work first to find the poor girl's body and then to discover how she met death."[14]

All through the month of May Mrs. Humiston and the private detectives in her employ looked in vain for clues concerning the whereabouts of the girl. Eventually they received information from several neighbors who swore they observed Cocchi, nervous and covered with dirt, leaving the basement of his shop late on the nights of February 13 and 14. A story related to her by Mrs. Louise LaRue, a client, finally

_____

14. "Mrs. Humiston, the Woman Who Shamed Police in the Ruth Cruger Murder Case," New York Times, 24 June 1917, Sec. VIII, p. 1.

7

convinced Mrs. Humiston to search Cocchi's cellar for the girl's body.
Mrs. LaRue claimed she was drugged, kidnapped, and held prisoner by a
band of white slave traders.[15] After escaping her captors, she told
her lawyer of seeing two other girls, plus the body of a dead girl,
which she believed to be the corpse of Ruth Cruger.[16]

Alfredo Cocchi's wife, however, refused to allow Mrs. Humiston to
examine the basement of the shop, but the woman soon sold the shop and
the new owner gladly gave the lady detective permission to dig up the
cellar. On June 16 workers revealed a section of the wooden cellar
floor, previously covered by a chest of drawers, which had been cut out.
Likewise, a section of the underlying concrete floor had been removed.
Digging through five feet of dirt, clothing, and motorcycle parts,
workers found the body of Ruth Cruger wrapped in a sheet of rubber. The
body was completely clothed and two pieces of nine-foot rope were tied
around her ankles and waist, presumably to lower her into the hole.[17]
An autopsy showed her skull had been crushed by a heavy object. Death
was caused by a knife wound found in the abdomen which extended to the
spinal column.[18] Two days after this discovery policemen found a trapdoor Cocchi had cut in the floor of the back room in his shop. They
theorized he had killed Ruth Cruger here and dropped the body through

---

15. "Mrs. LaRue Tells of Drug and Kidnappers," New York Times, 26
June 1917, p. 3.

16. This story was found by police to have been taken almost
exactly from a novel by Sax Rohmer entitled The Insidious Dr. Fu-Manchu,
which was a favorite of Mrs. LaRue.

17. "Find Ruth Cruger Buried in Cellar of Cocchi's Shop," New York
Times, 17 June 1917, Sec. I, p. 5.

18. "'Ripper's' Mark Found on Body of Ruth Cruger," New York Times,
18 June 1917, p. 1.

8

the trapdoor into the cellar below.[19]

Prior to this, Cocchi was found living with his parents in Bologna, Italy. The escape of a prime suspect to another country, and the failure to find the body in a basement detectives supposedly checked, left many questions to be answered by the police department. Police Commissioner Arthur Woods immediately launched an investigation into the possibility of police corruption. Information received by the District Attorney's office told of a number of policemen who were seen in conversation with Cocchi at his shop. It was learned Cocchi took bets on horse races at his motorcycle shop. In addition, it was believed he had acted as a collector of graft for motorcycle policemen in a system known as the "monkey-wrench game."[20] Because of this investigation, four policemen were suspended for taking bribes.

Meanwhile, federal authorities were making futile attempts to extradite Alfredo Cocchi from custody in Italy. Due to a statute of the Italian penal code forbidding the extradition of subjects wanted for crimes committed in foreign countries, the Italian government refused to release Cocchi to U.S. officials. The request was denied even after President Woodrow Wilson asked for his return to America. Nevertheless, Cocchi confessed to the murder of Ruth Cruger while in an Italian prison. He told authorities he tried to kiss her when she came back for her skates, but she attempted to escape. Angered by this, he struck her

---

19. The only entrance to the shop was by a flight of stairs located in front of the building. This meant to bury the body in the cellar Cocchi would have had to carry the body outside and down the steps. Instead, he was forced to saw a hole in the floor.

20. This was a method of graft in which drivers caught for speeding who wanted to avoid the consequences were told by policemen to go to Cocchi's repair shop and purchase a "monkey wrench" for $5, $10, $20, depending on the officer.

9

across the head with a wooden log.[21] Also in his confession he claimed

to have left home after the murder and spent two days and a night at

the home of a priest in New York City, who was later identified as

Father Gaspar Marretto. When his confession was completed, Cocchi re-

portedly told those around him that:

> An overpowering attraction for the young woman seized
> me. What happened afterward seems like a dream. . . . In
> view of the facts which have been presented, it must be
> true I attacked and killed her. But God help me, I didn't
> mean to. My will power could not resist anymore.[22]
> At last I feel relieved. I have freed myself from a
> nightmare which tortured my conscience. Now I have told
> everything, and I am ready to suffer any penalty.[23]

A trial was instituted in June, 1919, at Bologna concerning the

charge of murder against Cocchi. During the trial he claimed his wife

had actually killed the girl and he was only trying to protect her by

confessing. The court dismissed this as a last try to save himself.

Finally, on October 29, 1920, Alfredo Cocchi was convicted of the first

degree murder of Ruth Cruger and was sentenced to twenty-seven years

imprisonment in Italy. In addition, he was charged with attempted

criminal assault, falsifying passports, and false enrollment in the

military service.[24]

Although she modestly denied her part in the case, the total credit

was bestowed upon Mrs. Humiston. During a newspaper interview she

emphatically renounced the title of "Mrs. Sherlock Holmes" by commenting:

---

21. "Cocchi Confesses Killing Cruger Girl in a Jealous Rage,"
Philadelphia Inquirer, 24 June 1917, p. 1.

22. "Cocchi Tells How He Slew Ruth Cruger," *New York Times*, 26
June 1917, p. 3.

23. "Cocchi Confesses," p. 1.

24. "Cocchi Convicted, Gets 27 Years," *New York Times*, 30 October
1920, p. 1.

10

"I never read Sherlock Holmes. In fact, I am not a believer in deduction. Common sense and persistence will always solve a mystery. You never need theatricals nor Dr. Watsons if you stick to a case."[25]

Still, Mrs. Humiston was convinced Ruth Cruger had been a victim of a white slave organization and so she dedicated herself to the protection of the young girls in New York City and the "destruction of immorality." Offered a job as a Deputy Assistant District Attorney in June, 1917, she refused in favor of an unsalaried appointment as a special investigator under Police Commissioner Woods. Acting in this official post she investigated reports of missing girls until her dismissal in December. Her real goal at this time, though, was the establishment of an organization she called the Morality League of America. It was intended to distribute information regarding the white slave market and to look into tales of immorality. Under the leadership of a group of prominent New York citizens, large sums of money were accumulated in an account called the Ruth Cruger Emergency Fund, which was to support Mrs. Humiston in her hunt for missing women.

When asked to speak at a dinner for the Women Lawyers' Association on November 15, 1917, her zeal in condemning immorality proved to hurt her highly-held image and signaled the downfall of her career. In her address she made the following accusations against the United States Army:

> From statistics I have gathered I can say that at one
> of our big camps there are 600 girls who are about to be-
> come mothers who have no husbands. At Camp Upton located
> at Yaphank, Long Island, it has been reported to me, seven
> of these little mothers are dead.[26]

---

25. "Mrs. Humiston, the Woman Who Shamed Police," Sec. VIII, p. 1.

26. "Camp's Story Squelched," New York Times, 16 November 1917, p. 1.

11

These allegations came at the height of American involvement in
the war in Europe and thus were very unpopular with the Army and American public alike.

Upon being informed of the charges made against his camp and men,
Camp Upton's Commander Major General J. Franklin Bell repudiated any
knowledge of such conditions. An inquiry into Mrs. Humiston's accusations was soon enacted by the Army. She was asked by Raymond B. Fosdick,
chairman of the Committee on Army Morals, to present the evidence she
claimed to possess before a committee in Washington, D.C. This evidence
was never made public and the inquiry was dropped. The New York Times,
which had so often supported her work in the past, dismissed her claims
by suggesting she was being unwittingly used by German spies to circulate
rumors intended to weaken American patriotism.[27]

From this point on Grace Humiston was only given sporadic newspaper
coverage and was usually pictured as an eccentric anachronism. Her
attempt to form a social club for neighborhood youths resulted in her
arrest for operating a dance hall without a license. During the 1920s
she crusaded against illegal night clubs and claimed they received
police protection; again her allegations were ignored by a public that
saw Prohibition as nothing more than a minor inconvenience.

Even though newspapers make only minor references to her career
after 1926, it would probably be a mistake to assume Mrs. Humiston was
not active. Also, it should be noted that her life was not entirely
centered around her work. Once asked by a reporter if she preferred
her profession over home life she replied: "I prefer home--possibly
that sounds old-fashioned? Well, to me there's nothing like my

_____

27. "Accusations Made in Haste," New York Times, 19 November 1917,
p. 10.

12

home."[28] She was extremely devoted to her husband Howard and her friends and associates. Despite the fact that women lawyers were a rarity in her day and age, her personal life helps to show why she remained neutral when it came to the question of women's rights.

When Mrs. Humiston died (on July 16, 1948) at the age of seventy-seven, most of America had long forgotten her major cases and her contributions to the betterment of society. Those who read her obituary never realized the effect she had upon the lives of so many people in the first quarter of the twentieth century. Few have shown the sympathy and humanitarian concern for others that Mrs. Humiston made her self-assumed task.

---

28. "Mrs. Humiston, the Woman Who Shamed Police," Sec. VIII, p. 1.

13

WORKING BIBLIOGRAPHY

"Absolves Stielow, Who Will Be Freed." New York Times, 9 May 1918,
        p. 1.

"Accusations Made in Haste." (Editorial), New York Times, 19 November
        1917, p. 10.

"Asks Mrs. Humiston to Find Girls." New York Times, 17 September 1917,
        p. 13.

"Asks Police to Find Daughter." New York Times, 15 February 1917, p. 11.

"Called for Trial 43 Times." New York Times, 8 August 1921, p. 13.

"Camp's Story Squelched." New York Times, 16 November 1917, pp. 1, 6.

"Captain Turns on Mrs. Humiston." New York Times, 26 June 1919, p. 15.

"Case of Ruth Cruger, The." (Editorial), New York Times, 18 June 1918,
        p. 8.

"Charles Stielow." (Editorial), Independent, 21 August 1916, p. 258.

"Clears Mrs. Humiston." New York Times, 16 July 1919, p. 13.

"Cocchi Confesses Killing Cruger Girl in a Jealous Rage." Philadelphia
        Inquirer, 24 June 1917, pp. 1, 2.

"Cocchi Convicted, Gets 27 Years." New York Times, 30 October 1920,
        p. 1.

"Cocchi Found in Italy." New York Times, 1 June 1917, p. 10.

"Cocchi Now Accuses His Wife of Murder." New York Times, 25 June 1919,
        p. 8.

"Cocchi on Trial for Cruger Murder." New York Times, 26 October 1920,
        p. 18.

"Cocchi Tells How He Slew Ruth Cruger." New York Times, 26 June 1917,
        p. 3.

"Cocchi Took Bets at His Cycle Shop." New York Times, 7 July 1917,
        p. 16.

"Compromise Highly Unsatisfactory." New York Times, 5 December 1916,
        p. 10.

"Condemned Man Has Child's Brain." New York Times, 11 July 1916, p. 6.

14

"Confess Double Murder." New York Times, 24 April 1915, p. 7.

"Decided Stielow Must Die." New York Times, 27 July 1916, p. 18.

"Detective Freed on Court's Order." New York Times, 5 August 1921, p. 7.

"Detective Under the Harrow." (Editorial), New York Times, 30 June 1917, p. 101.

"Dig for Cruger Clues." New York Times, 13 June 1917, p. 22.

"Dr. Straton Heard By Federal Jury." New York Times, 8 April 1920, p. 17.

"Dr. Straton Tells of Buying Drinks." New York Times, 5 April 1920, p. 17.

"Doomed to Die, Spurns Aid." New York Times, 10 June 1920, p. 16.

"Drawing Morals Where None Are to Be Found." (Editorial), New York Times, 18 July 1917, p. 8.

"Escapes Execution; Family Before Cell." New York Times, 13 June 1926, Sec. I, p. 20.

"Fails to Indict King." New York Times, 22 December 1917, p. 5.

"Feminine 'Sherlock Holmes,' A." The Literary Digest, 7 July 1917, p. 50.

"Find Ruth Cruger Buried in Cellar of Cocchi's Shop." New York Times, 17 June 1917, Sec. I, pp. 1, 5.

"Find Trapdoor Used by Slayer in Cruger Murder." New York Times, 19 June 1917, p. 1.

"Forms Morality League." New York Times, 8 August 1917, p. 7.

"Friction Over Missing Girl." New York Times, 19 February 1917, p. 12.

"Girl Drugged, Father Says." New York Times, 20 February 1917, p. 20.

"Girl Kidnapped, Fear of Father." Philadelphia Inquirer, 16 February 1917, p. 7.

Goldman, Mayer C. "The Stielow Case." The New Republic, 18 January 1919, p. 343.

"Governor Saves Life of Stielow." New York Times, 4 December 1916, p. 6.

"Grace Humiston Run Over by Truck." New York Times, 15 March 1923, p. 21.

15

"Her Triumph Condemns Their Failure." (Editorial), New York Times, 19
    June 1917, p. 12.

"Hunt Missing Man Miss Cruger Knew." New York Times, 17 February 1917,
    p. 6.

"Hylan and Enright Demand Vice List." New York Times, 6 March 1920,
    p. 24.

"Indict Detective for Graft: Police Vice Ring Alleged." New York
    Times, 4 March 1920, pp. 1, 6.

"King Now Retracts Murder Confession." New York Times, 15 August 1916,
    p. 5.

"King Says Another Murdered Phelps." New York Times, 12 August 1916,
    p. 18.

"King Under Arrest: Before Grand Jury." New York Times, 14 December
    1917, p. 14.

"King Under Arrest for Phelps Murder." New York Times, 13 August 1916,
    Sec. I, p. 5.

"Mrs. Humiston Denies Police Attack." New York Times, 21 July 1918,
    p. 12.

"Mrs. Humiston Fears Trap." New York Times, 22 September 1921, p. 6.

"Mrs. Humiston, 77, Crime Lawyer Dies." New York Times, 18 July 1948,
    p. 52.

"Mrs. Humiston, the Woman Who Shamed Police in the Ruth Cruger Murder
    Case." New York Times, 24 June 1917, Sec. VIII, p. 1.

"Mrs. LaRue Tells of Drug and Kidnappers." New York Times, 26 June
    1917, p. 3.

"Mrs. LaRue's Tale is Found in a Novel." New York Times, 24 July 1917,
    p. 9.

"New Clue in Cruger Case." New York Times, 22 February 1917, p. 13.

"New Ruth Cruger Clue." New York Times, 24 February 1917, p. 16.

"Object to Girls' Club." New York Times, 26 August 1917, p. 5.

"$1,000,000 to Save Women." New York Times, 24 August 1917, p. 9.

"Open New Fight to Save Stielow." New York Times, 28 September 1916,
    p. 7.

"Police Puzzled by Girl Who Vanished." New York Times, 9 July 1917,
    p. 9.

16

"Police Were Deaf to Pleas of Sister." New York Times, 26 June 1917, p. 3.

"Prosecutor Asks Aid as a Deputy of Mrs. Humiston." New York Times, 29 June 1917, pp. 1, 4.

"Question Priest on Cocchi's Tale of Getting Aid." New York Times, 26 June 1917, p. 1.

"'Ripper's' Mark Found on Body of Ruth Cruger." New York Times, 18 June 1917, pp. 1, 3.

"Ruth Cruger Fund and Mrs. Humiston." New York Times, 16 August 1917, p. 22.

"Say King Can Show Alibi." New York Times, 17 August 1916, p. 7.

"Says No to Mrs. Humiston." New York Times, 25 July 1917, p. 20.

"Sherlock Appears at Last in Real Life." (Editorial), New York Times, 26 June 1917, p. 12.

"Shoots Man to Death in Husband's Presence." New York Times, 5 March 1905, p. 11.

"Slayers' Pleas Heard." New York Times, 6 April 1926, p. 31.

"Smith Hears Pleas for Condemned Men." New York Times, 4 June 1926, p. 4.

"Stielow Champion Seeks Real Slayer." New York Times, 19 July 1916, p. 17.

"Stielow May Go Free: Another Confesses." New York Times, 11 August 1916, p. 18.

"Stielow Released from Auburn Prison." New York Times, 10 May 1918, p. 6.

"Stielow Reprieved on Verge of Death." New York Times, 30 July 1916, Sec. I, p. 11.

"Strange Case of Charles F. Stielow." New York Times, 12 June 1918, Sec. IV, p. 5.

"Suspect Policeman in the Cruger Case." New York Times, 4 March 1917, Sec. I, p. 14.

"Takes Police Power from Mrs. Humiston." New York Times, 30 December 1917, Sec. II, p. 3.

"Two Sentenced to Die." New York Times, 29 June 1915, p. 9.

"Upholds Baptist Pastor." New York Times, 1 March 1921, p. 2.

17

"Urge Wilson to Ask the King for Cocchi." New York Times, 13 July 1917, p. 18.

White, Frank Marshall. "Where There Are Women There's a Way." Good Housekeeping, August 1918, pp. 54 et passim.

"Woman Guilty of Murder." New York Times, 27 April 1905, p. 5.

"Woman May Save Stielow." New York Times, 18 July 1916, p. 9.

"Women Give Evidence Against a Detective." New York Times, 4 August 1921, p. 8.

"Won't Aid Fosdick in Camp Inquiry." New York Times, 17 November 1917, p. 18.

"Woods Enlists Aid of Mrs. Humiston." New York Times, 22 July 1917, Sec. I, p. 9.

"Would Reopen Cocchi Case." New York Times, 27 June 1919, p. 20.

THE MURDER OF RED CASSIDY

by Vicki Kant

Although the 1920s in America are sometimes referred to as the "Dry
Decade," in reality the period was a "sopping wet farce."[1] Prohibition,
that "noble experiment," was undermined by a thirsty public kept supplied
by bootleggers who smuggled alcoholic beverages to night clubs in every
major city. "Blind pigs," as bars were sometimes called, ended up as
social gathering places made all the more attractive because they were
illegal. Here socialites and gangsters mixed easily as "thousands of
speakeasies spangled the city like dandelions in spring."[2]

One of the better-known speakeasies in New York City (at least to
police) was the Hotsy-Totsy Club, an establishment partially owned by
gangsters and one that attracted various underworld figures. It was
here on July 13, 1929, that William "Red" Cassidy, a small time hoodlum,
and Simon Walker, an ex-convict, were shot to death in a beer brawl
which in a sense vividly portrays the temper of times.

On the night of this double slaying the club was doing a brisk
business as usual. At 3:45 a.m., Red Cassidy, a well-known beer runner,
along with his brother Peter and a few others, staggered into the club
after they had been drinking elsewhere.[3] At one end of the bar a group

---

1. Paul Sann, The Lawless Decade (New York: Crown Publishers,
1957), p. 7.

2. Kenneth Allsop, The Bootleggers and Their Era (New Rochelle,
N.Y.: Arlington House, 1968), p. 32.

3. "Two Shot to Death in Night Club Row," New York Times, 14 July
1929, p. 20.

2

of men sat drinking beer. Peter Cassidy went to the counter and "asked for service by banging on the bar with his ham-hock fists and shouting: 'C'mon you punks give me some goddamn service.'"[4] A group of men at the other end of the bar were "annoyed with Cassidy's rudeness" and stood up to defend the bartender. It was then that Peter Cassidy "made disparaging remarks" about one man's ability as a boxer and shouted: "Where I come from the middle name is fight."[5] Simon Walker, who was seated on the far side of the club started toward Peter Cassidy with his pistol drawn, but Red Cassidy jumped up and grabbed the gun. More words were exchanged between the two groups, then almost instantly "the small barroom roared with a fusillade of shots" and forty patrons rushed outside to escape the battle.

The police arrived several minutes later and fought to quiet the crowd that had gathered in front of the club. When they finally got inside they found thirty-eight year old Simon Walker shot to death and thirty year old Peter Cassidy, "a redoubtable brawler," wounded from a bullet that had grazed the top of his head. Red Cassidy had already been rushed to the hospital with three bullets in his head, one in the abdomen, and one in the groin. He was conscious briefly but when detectives attempted to question him "his only response was a curse."[6] He died approximately one hour later. Police rounded up twenty-five people as possible witnesses and seven were held for further questioning. Also, thirty bottles of ale, one half keg of beer and one half bottle of whiskey were confiscated from the club.

---

4. Jay Robert Nash, _Bloodletters and Badmen_ (New York: M. Evans and Company, 1973), p. 156.

5. "Two Shot to Death in Night Club Row," p. 20.

6. _Ibid_.

3

On July 16, 1929, Red Cassidy's funeral was held at the Calvary Cemetery. His body was carried from his home in a solid bronze, silver trimmed coffin. Three carloads of flowers were sent to Cassidy's mother and fifty cars filled with mourners followed the white hearse as it paraded through the gangster's home territory. "About a dozen detectives attended the services, with glances darting from face to face as they looked for gunmen and under world characters."[7] Peter Cassidy was unable to attend the service because he was being held as a material witness. Mrs. Bridget Cassidy, mother of the deceased clung to her other son and sobbed quietly while Cassidy's widow and two year old daughter stood nearby.[8]

A few days later John (Legs) Diamond, notorious gunman and part owner of the Hotsy-Totsy Club, along with Charles Entratta, his body guard, were both indicted for first degree murder. Police Commissioner Whalen who issued the order declared: "this will serve as a message to gangdom that the police will give them no quarter."[9] However, both men eluded police, and it was not until late August that Chicago police found Entratta hiding out with his wife Anna. As Entratta was led away he asked his wife for money to buy cigarettes and she casually pulled out a roll of money worth $1,200 and handed her husband a one dollar bill. When questioned neither Entratta nor his wife would discuss the murder unless police supplied positive proof that he was even in New

---

7. "Bury Beer Runner in Gangland Pomp," New York Times, 17 July 1929, p. 27. Police admitted they did not find anyone, "although there were a few 'bad eggs' at the funeral . . . and pointed to limousines with drawn shades."

8. Ibid.

9. "Police Arrest 81 in Midtown Raid," New York Times, 21 July 1929, p. 8.

4

York the night of July 13.[10] Police had even less luck getting information from Legs Diamond. It wasn't until well into March that he gave himself up, marching into the station house and announcing to James Donnelly, a New York detective: "I hear you want me. Well I'm here to surrender."[11] He would not answer any questions.

Then on August 25, 1929, "three of the men who saw murders in the Hotsy-Totsy Club when the dawn of July 13 was enfeebling the lights of Broadway . . . ," were reported dead.[12] Hymie Cohen, the entertainment manager of the club, one unknown waiter, and a waiter identified as "William Wolgast" were the victims. Commissioner Whalen sarcastically stated that Cohen apparently saw the entire murder from start to finish, and when the argument got louder "the vigilant Cohen, in an effort to keep the picturesque language from the tender ears of those to be found in a speakeasy at 3 a.m., ordered the orchestra to play up."[13] His death, along with the others, made Entratta's eventual trial a farce.

On August 28, 1929, Charles Entratta, better known as "Charlie Green" among New York racketeers, was arraigned before Judge Mulqueen. His trial opened in early February and Assistant District Attorney William B. Moore claimed the murders were not the result of a feud between midtown beer runners, but were due to a "sneering remark" made by Peter Cassidy to Ruby Goldstein, a boxer and witness to the double killing. This was all supposition on Moore's part and proving his theory

---

10. "Entratta Seized in Chicago," New York Times, 25 August 1929, p. 10.

11. "Diamond Gives Up in Cabaret Murders," New York Times, 11 March 1930, p. 29.

12. "Murder Witnesses Slain, Says Whalen," New York Times, 27 August 1929, p. 29.

13. "Murder Witnesses Slain," p. 29.

5

was very difficult because his four key witnesses turned out to be use-less. Three of the witnesses (Ruby Goldstein, a boxer; Nathaniel Jarvis, a friend of Goldstein's; and Peter Cassidy) all said they were in the club at the time of the shooting but claimed they did not know who fired the shots. Chief medical examiner Doctor Thomas A. Gonzales testified that Red was killed with a .38 calibre pistol and Simon Walker was shot from a .32 calibre weapon.[14] Twenty-two year old Goldstein confirmed District Attorney Moore's theory about how the brawl began, but he dis-played considerable uneasiness on the stand and told the court that he hid with some forty other people behind the orchestra platform and did not see the actual shooting. Jarvis's testimony was similar to Gold-stein's, and Peter Cassidy stated that he was too drunk to notice who did the actual shooting. Cassidy did say though that his brother Red told him Legs Diamond was one of the bartenders that night, but this was as close a connection to Diamond as police ever found.

Luke Reilly, the doorman on duty the night of the double murder, shed new light on the killings when he gave his testimony. He stated that an unknown bartender fled from the club "stuffing a pistol into his trouser's pocket a few seconds after the shooting."[15] Reilly said that Cohen, the manager, ran down and told him to open the doors because a fight was going on. Shortly after this he spotted the new bartender running across the road trying to put the "blue steel" pistol into his hip pocket. The doorman's testimony went no further than this because District Attorney Moore felt that an investigation was in order and a

---

14. "Three Deny Seeing Night Club Slayer," *New York Times*, 7 February 1929, p. 13.

15. "Gives New Version of Cafe Murders," *New York Times*, 8 February 1929, p. 17.

6

two-day adjournment was obtained.[16]

When the trial resumed Moore put Tony Merola,[17] a singing waiter
and violinist, on the stand. Merola had been held as a material witness
and it was believed he would be able to identify both Entratta and Diamond as the murderers. Early in August, Merola's wife had issued an
application for his release as a witness because she felt he was becoming unbalanced and should be sent to a psychopathic ward.[18] His release
was opposed by District Attorney Moore who believed Merola was merely
suffering from "stage fright" about the trial. When Merola appeared on
the stand, George Z. Medalie (Entratta's lawyer) claimed the witness was
not of sound mind and requested a medical examination. Judge Rosalsky
became insensed at this move and stated:

> This is the first time since I came to the bench in
> 1894 that the mental capacity of a witness has been ques-
> tioned in this way during a trial. This did not even
> happen in the Harry K. Thaw murder trials.[19]

Dr. Israel S. Wechler, an "alienist" connected with Columbia University,
held that Merola was legally sane because he had an "understanding of
his actions" and thus Tony Merola gave his testimony as planned. But
after all this legal maneuvering he simply told the court that he, like
the others, saw nothing because he hid when the firing began. At this
point Judge Rosalsky pronounced a not guilty verdict even before

---

16. It was reported that a search was put into effect for this
unknown bartender but police believed he was one of the three victims
reportedly slain in late August.

17. Merola's first name was also printed as "Thomas" and "John."

18. "Refuses to Free Merola," New York Times, 6 August 1929, p.
28.

19. "Gives New Version of Cafe Murders," p. 17.

7

Entratta's lawyer requested it.[20] Entratta was set free but just as he left the courtroom he was picked up and charged with a violation of parole and was sent back to prison for eleven years.[21]

The trial of John "Legs" Diamond began shortly after Entratta's trial ended. Diamond, who received his nickname because he was once a dancer, had worked his way up from a bodyguard to a powerful gang lord. Diamond also pleaded not guilty and defied officials in every possible way before his trial. Diamond had told police that he was a "clerk," and Chief Mulrooney's reply to this statement was: "Outside of being a clerk and a murderer, what other occupations have you had."[22] (Diamond's only reaction to this remark was a smile.) Diamond further annoyed the police when he was asked to appear in a line-up because it was believed he was also involved in a robbery in Newark, New Jersey. Diamond refused to leave his cell, claiming that he knew his rights. Mrs. Deckel, a woman witness in the hold-up, was then taken to Diamond's cell to identify him. Diamond defiantly lay down on his cot and put his face under the pillow until his "visitors" got tired of waiting.

At the outset of Diamond's trial his lawyer produced two witnesses who swore he was in Massachusetts the morning of the murder. Because the prosecution's vital witnesses were all dead or saw nothing, the outcome of the trial was predictable.[23] Diamond was freed on the murder

---

20. "Greene Acquitted in Cafe Murders," New York Times, 11 February 1930, p. 29.

21. Ibid.

22. "Bail Refused Diamond in Killing," New York Times, 12 March 1930, p. 31.

23. A fourth man, Henry Herman, was also sought as a witness, but he had been killed in an unrelated shooting in Philadelphia.

8

charge but was immediately rearrested for a drug smuggling charge.[24]

In late March of 1930, the New York police went to New Jersey to find Alexander Martin, since he was thought to have been in the Hotsy-Totsy Club the evening of the murders. Martin told police he was wounded during the fight as an innocent bystander. However, nothing came of his testimony and this was the last mention of the double slaying in the Hotsy-Totsy Club and the case was left unsolved due to lack of evidence.

In the final analysis one tends to discount the story of the mysterious bartender, and it is also hard to believe that Diamond and Entratta were the murderers as Jay Robert Nash and others assume.[25] It is far easier to believe that these killings were the result of a tavern brawl just as the District Attorney outlined and the fact that the men were killed with different guns tends to support this. Still, police must be faulted for their handling of the investigation, and bringing the case to trial with so little evidence seemed simply to be an attempt to pacify an outraged public. On the other hand Jack Diamond took no chances, and as happened so many times during that era, the underworld proved to be more organized and efficient than the police. The fact that both Diamond and Entratta fled New York after the double slaying and that Diamond surrendered after eight months when all the witnesses were dead, is certainly suspicious; however, this would have been a natural reaction on the part of these gangsters. Because the killings occurred in Diamond's club he would not want to be charged, mistakenly

---

24. "Rearrest Diamond After His Release," New York Times, 22 March 1930, p. 10.

25. Jay Robert Nash, "Diamond, John Thomas" in Bloodletters and Badmen (New York: M. Evans and Company, 1973), p. 156-157.

9

or otherwise, and so skipped town. Although it was reported that three murder witnesses were themselves killed, only one body was found and this could have been done as "insurance" in case Diamond and his bodyguard were brought to trial.

10

WORKING BIBLIOGRAPHY

Allsop, Kenneth. The Bootleggers and Their Era. New Rochelle, New
     York: Arlington Press House, 1968.

"Bury Beer Runner in Gangland Pomp." New York Times, 4 September 1929,
     p. 31.

"Diamond Declared a Fugitive by Court." New York Times, 20 July 1929,
     p. 31.

"Diamond and Entratta Indicted on Murder Charge." New York Times, 20
     July 1929, p. 1, 63.

"Diamond Gives Up in Cabaret Murders." New York Times, 11 March 1930,
     p. 29.

"Entratta Denies Guilt." New York Times, 29 August 1929, p. 26.

"Gives New Version of Cafe Murders." New York Times, 8 February 1930,
     p. 17.

"Greene Aquitted in Cafe Murders." New York Times, 11 February 1930,
     p. 29.

"Green Here, Denies Cabaret Killings." New York Times, 28 August 1929,
     p. 9.

"Green's Trial Opens in Double Murder." New York Times, 6 February
     1930, p. 25.

"Indictment Returned in Night Club Killing." New York Times, 19 July
     1929, p. 22.

"Murder Witnesses Slain, Says Whalen." New York Times, 27 August 1929,
     p. 29.

Nash, Jay Robert, Bloodletters and Badmen, New York: M. Evans and
     Company, 1973, pp. 153-159.

"Police Say They Know Night Club Killers." New York Times, 16 July
     1929, p. 26.

"Queried in Killings Here and Hoboken." New York Times, 23 March 1930,
     p. 21.

"Rearrest Diamond After His Release." New York Times, 22 March 1930,
     p. 10.

"Refuses to Free Merola." New York Times, 6 August 1929, p. 28.

11

"Rothstein Named in 5 Feud Murders." New York Times, 22 March 1930, p. 1.

Sann, Paul. The Lawless Decade. New York, Crown Publishers, 1957.

"Seized in Chicago for Two Killings Here." New York Times, 25 August 1929, p. 10.

"Three Deny Seeing Night Club Slayer." New York Times, 7 February 1930, p. 13.

"Two Shot to Death in Night Club Row." New York Times, 14 July 1929, p. 20.

THE COCOS ISLAND TREASURE EXPEDITIONS

by Grant Mahon

The lure of buried pirate gold has attracted many treasure seekers
throughout the years, but none has proved more enticing than the rumor
of hidden wealth--some one hundred million dollars in gold--which supposedly lies on Cocos Island, a remote speck of land southwest of Costa
Rica. Located some five hundred miles off the western coast of Panama,
in the tropical seas of the Pacific Ocean, Cocos Island is an uninhabited
land mass of approximately fourteen square miles. During the age of
exploration, the tiny island provided fresh water for passing sailors,
but it also became a perfect treasure trove for pirates who looted
Spanish galleons along the Latin American coast.

Supposedly, the pirates Edward Davis, Sir Henry Morgan, Lionel
Wafer, and a Scotsman known only as "Thompson," used this "minute dot in
the Pacific" as a storage place for their stolen treasures.[1]

The first of these buccaneers to make use of the solitary island as
a safekeeping for his plundered riches was Davis. After filling the
hull of his ship with Spanish gold from galleons sailing along the west
coast of South America, he went to Cocos and, according to a "writing
man" on board the vessel, "beached his ship, cleaned her bottom, re-
rigged her, and buried his treasure."[2]

---

1. Other treasures were mentioned, but research provided no further information, and this author is skeptical about their existence.

2. Morton Savell, "Cocos Island Perenial Goal of Treasure Seekers,"
Literary Digest, 14 April 1934, p. 42.

2

In 1671, Sir Henry Morgan, with a force of 2,200 men and 37 vessels, sacked Panama City.[3] The vast treasures from Peru and Mexico that were awaiting shipment to Europe were loaded aboard Morgan's ships and then the Welsh buccaneer left the city in burning ruins. He is alleged to have taken the treasure and buried it, in part, on Cocos.[4] More treasure was supposedly left there when the English surgeon-pirate, Lionel Wafer, buried loot on Cocos in 1710.[5]

But over and above any of this wealth was the "Loot of Lima," secured on the island by a Scottish pirate known as Captain Thompson. Thompson had put ashore in the harbor of Callo, in Peru, in 1824 at about the same time that Simon Bolivar was in the process of liberating the country from Spanish rule. Lima was Spain's wealthiest city in the New World, and city officials feared the treasure would fall into the hands of the rebels. So, they loaded the most valuable of their riches (including two gold Madonnas from the Lima Cathedral) aboard Thompson's ship, the <u>Mary Dear</u>, and then went aboard themselves, assuming the rebels would not dare attack a "ship of the British flag." But officials did not reckon on the Scot and his crew murdering them in their sleep and putting out to sea to bury the gold on Cocos.[6]

Months later the <u>Mary Dear</u> was captured and the crew executed, but Thompson escaped, and, for almost twenty-five years he sailed and pirated the same area with one Benito Benito, also known as "Benito of the Bloody

---

3. "Morgan, Sir Henry," <u>Cyclopedia of Names</u>, Vol. 2, 1954.

4. "President Goes Fishing and Spins Pirate Yarns," <u>New York Times</u>, 24 February 1940, p. 7.

5. <u>Ibid</u>.

6. "Cocos Island a Place of Fabled Treasure," <u>New York Times</u>, 31 January 1932, sec. 5, p. 19.

3

Sword."[7] Eventually he became partners with a man named Keating and
together they engaged a Captain Bogue[8] and made plans to recover the
Peruvian gold that Thompson had buried on Cocos. However, Thompson died
before the expedition could get underway and so the treasure map was
left in the hands of the other two. After this, the crew mutinied;
"Bogue was drowned on Cocos, and Keating barely escaped with his life
before the treasure could be removed."[9]

This was the earliest of many unsuccessful attempts to discover the
treasure of Cocos Island, but one hundred years later a number of treasure expeditions set out to find the fabled gold.

The first of these expeditions was that of the Clayton Metalphone
Company, Ltd., out of Vancouver, British Columbia, in 1931.[10] One year
earlier, under the name of the "Cocos Island Treasure Company, Ltd.,"
the Clayton Metalphone Company was granted all rights to search for
treasure on the island by the Costa Rican government, with the concession that the Republic receive a percentage of all finds.[11]

The company, under the command of Colonel J. E. Leckie, felt their
chances of discovering treasures buried in past centuries was extremely
good for two reasons: One, they possessed maps "with an 'X' marked on

---

7. Savell, p. 42.

8. Bogue's name was also spelled "Boag" but the first spelling was
more prevalent throughout the research material and is therefore used in
this paper.

9. Savell, p. 42. Keating confessed on his deathbed that he and
Bogue had found the Lima gold and that he had killed Bogue himself.
However, Keating was forced to leave the island before the treasure
could be removed.

10. "Cocos Island Gold to be Sought Again," New York Times, 22
November 1931, sec. 3, p. 6.

11. Ibid.

4

the spots where pieces of eight, Inca gold and priceless jewels may be awaiting discovery"; and two, they carried a device called the Clayton Metalphone, which was capable of detecting metals under the earth or in water.[12]

Their ship, the Silver Wave, left Vancouver on February 22, 1932, with twenty-five men. Under the provisions of the treasure contract of 1930, they could remain on the island until October 1932, but could then renew the lease if necessary.[13]

From the outset, the tropical growth proved a hindrance to the men as they tried to survey the island. There were marks of previous expeditions --empty holes and numerous tunnels in the sides of mountains--but the "amazing metalphone" only seemed to work near the shoreline. Surveys of Cocos proved of little avail and persistent rain made conditions insufferable.

Throughout July, reports of treasure finds and then reports denying those finds were transmitted.[14] In one message, after a denial of discovery, the expedition's radio operator said: "How did anyone ever get the notion we would find anything on this God-forsaken island?"[15] Another member, Lieutenant Dennis Rooke, stated that "members of the expedition were nearly starved and were forced to subsist on wild pig meat and coconuts."[16] Colonel Leckie denied their accusations and explained that,

---

12. Ibid.

13. "Vancouver Treasure Hunters Leave for Cocos Isle," New York Times, 22 February 1932, p. 35.

14. "Devonshire Treasure Reportedly Discovered," New York Times, 6 July 1932, p. 19.

15. "Treasure Discovery Denied," New York Times, 7 July 1932, p. 19.

16. "Cocos Island Treasure Hunters Report They Are Still on Job," New York Times, 24 July 1932, p. 9.

5

> Rooke was only on the island a short time. The party
> was on shore rations for a few days while awaiting the
> arrival of a supply ship, but there was never any hard-
> ship or anxiety, nor has there been a single man sick.
> Any talk of dissention is pure rot. . . . We have an
> excellent chance of success.[17]

But four months later, on Christmas day, the Vancouver party left Cocos Island, after several million dollars had been put into a "fruitless expedition."[18] No glittering gold or brilliant jewels were found and the expedition, like so many others before them, returned home a total failure.

Apparently publicity concerning the expedition was an inspiration to other groups, and despite the failure of the Clayton Metalphone Company, a group of Britons decided to recover the riches of Cocos in 1934. Promoted by Captain Charles Arthur, the Treasury Recovery Company, Ltd., sailed for the island with the same high hopes as those before them.

> This is the first scientific treasure hunt. Our experts
> will tackle it as an engineering problem. We have definite
> evidence as to where the treasure is buried. . . . We are
> using an airplane for surveying purposes.[19]

Unfortunately, the group overlooked an important item--they failed to obtain proper authorization from Costa Rica.[20] Consequently, the Republic arranged for the immediate deportation of the treasure hunters,

---

17. "Reports of Hardship on Cocos Isle Denied," *New York Times*, 25 July 1932, p. 2.

18. "Treasure Hunters Tire of Wild Pig Diet," *New York Times*, 25 December 1932, p. 6.

19. "Engineers to Seek Cocos Island Gold," *New York Times*, 16 September 1934, p. 4.

20. In England, the Treasury Recovery Company was told the island was not internationally recognized as Costa Rica's. Costa Rica claimed they sent the expedition a message in Panama saying they would be arrested if they landed on the island, but the expedition claimed they never received such a message and went ahead.

6

and sent fifty national policemen to the island with orders to "overcome any resistance. . . ."[21]

While the treasure seekers were being rounded up, Commander Frank Worsley, the Captain of the ship, radioed an apology to Costa Rican President Jimenez while Arthur returned to England with the excuse of obtaining a larger vessel for the company.[22] Eventually, the entire expedition, with the exception of Arthur, was arrested and ended up in Costa Rica for trial. Costa Rica confiscated the equipment but released the men in late October, after members of the group testified that Arthur was the sole promoter of the company and "they were only the servants of the promoters."[23] They arrived in England in January, two months after Costa Rica renewed its Cocos Island contract with the Clayton Metalphone Company.[24]

This, however, did not stop the British search for gold. Worsley and the chairman of the Treasury Recovery Company, Erik Hankey, made arrangements with Costa Rica for an authorized search of the island in February, 1935.[25]

On April 5, 1935, Costa Rica gave an official authorization and British Tours, Ltd. (the old Treasury Recovery Company) tried to raise funds in England. Their ship, the Veracity, again under the command of

---

21. "Treasure Hunters Held," New York Times, 14 October 1934, p. 2.

22. "Treasure Hunters Offer Apology," New York Times, 15 October 1934, p. 6.

23. "Treasure Hunters May Go Free Today," New York Times, 29 November 1934, p. 6.

24. "Gold Seekers Go Home," New York Times, 14 November 1934, p. 8.

25. Apparently, Costa Rica gave in to Hankey's offer of one-third of any find.

7

Worsley, reached the Canal Zone in early June, along with a Belgian, Peter Bergmanns, who was shipwrecked on Cocos in 1929 and claimed he had discovered the "treasure cache." He had been offered a quarter of any discovery for his help.[26] A force of ten Costa Rican policemen was waiting to sail from Puntarenas, Costa Rica, with the expedition to protect the Republic's share in the project.[27]

Finally, on June 7, 1935, the *Veracity* sailed from Puntarenas with a ten-man police detail and a crew of fifteen under the command of Worsley and his assistant, Commander F. C. Finnis. Their contract provided for the group to stay on Cocos until October.

Still the British could not seem to keep themselves out of trouble. Before they even got to Cocos, the crew complained because they had not been paid for their services since they left England. They were upset over the fact that Arthur still had control over the operation, from Balboa, and when his cousin, Richard Studdert, arrived from England and took charge, insult was added to injury.

By September the expedition was near mutiny, having not received a penny of their salary, and Costa Rica made arrangements with the commanders of the expedition to remove the police force on the isle only if the men abandoned the entire project.

Then, on October 30, 1935, Costa Rican Congressman Carlos Jimenez (not the president) heatedly accused British Tours, Ltd., of selling stock to the English public in the name of Costa Rica, for the "unlikely" discovery of treasure on Cocos. "He alleged the company's financial

---

26. "Treasure Hunt Ends," *New York Times*, 11 March 1936, p. 21.

27. Arthur, still the main promoter, remained in Balboa fearing arrest if he went to the island. ("Costa Rica Gives Permit for British Treasure Hunt," *New York Times*, 5 April 1935, p. 4.)

8

operations in London were fraudulent and urged the president to cancel the concession."[28]

By November 15, the charter for the Veracity was cancelled for the expedition "because of the lack of funds."[29] After this, things seemed to settle down until February 1936, and then Costa Rica ordered the complete evacuation of the isle because of the expedition's failure to come up with "compensation funds" for the government. The order was repealed when "last minute" funds arrived from England to take care of the "overdue obligations," but the president declared that "no matter what," the concession would end in April and the expedition must leave the island.

Finally, in March, the hunt came to an end when Bergmanns disappeared. Most of the expedition left Cocos to await a return voyage to England and appealed to the British Foreign Ministry for the salaries they never received after Captain Hardy MacMahon, the company's representative in Costa Rica, announced that of the $200,000 collected in England, only one-tenth had been spent on the expedition, the rest going to "administrators in London."[30]

In May 1936, the four remaining members of the group on the island were retrieved and the "destitute British" started their return journey to England.

But perhaps the most bizarre search for the legendary treasure was

---

28. President Jimenez had extended the concession until April before the congressman's attack. ("Assails Treasure Hunt," New York Times, 30 October 1935, p. 10.)

29. "Cocos Isle Police Squad Sends Appeal for Food," New York Times, 26 November 1935, p. 18.

30. "Cocos Treasure Search Ends as Permit Expires," New York Times, 21 April 1936, p. 19.

9

the one undertaken by Benjamin "Bugsy" Siegel, the notorious gangster.
Sometime in 1937, the racketeer heard there were millions in Spanish
treasure buried on the island "from the famous wreck of the Mary Dear"
and he and a "Damon Runyon" crew set out after it.[31] Siegel told his
"crew" they were "gonna grab the stuff and then beat it . . . and then
we're all gonna go home rich."[32] Dressed in a "stylish pinstripe suit
and pointed two-tone shoes," Siegel's idea of blasting for treasure was
hurling hand grenades into the jungle. After a few weeks they gave up
on their venture and sailed for Europe in an attempt to sell munitions
to Mussolini.

So, after one hundred years and more than eighty expeditions, abso-
lutely nothing in the way of treasure has been found--and one wonders
if there is anything there to be found. When one looks at the various
expeditions of the 1930s, it is easy to see why they all failed. The
Clayton Metalphone Company had perhaps the best chance but it is doubt-
ful that the detector was very effective, especially when it was reported that it registered metals in an area where digging yielded
nothing.[33] (It could just have easily failed to register metals where
they really were.) Finally, even though Colonel Leckie stated otherwise,
the crews were in bad spirits and did not work very effectively.

In the case of the British expeditions, it would appear that the
promoters were not interested in discovering treasure at all. Instead,
they wanted to extract as much money as they could from the sale of

---

31. Jay Robert Nash, Bloodletters and Badmen (New York: M. Evans
and Co., 1973), p. 503. Nash probably confuses Thompson's ship, the
Mary Dear, with a novel by Hammond Innes, The Wreck of the Mary Deare
which had nothing to do with Cocos Island.

32. Ibid.

33. "Devonshire Treasure Reportedly Discovered," p. 35.

10

stock of a company that had already planned to fail. This hypothesis is strongly supported by the statement of Captain MacMahon, and the fact that members of the expedition never received their salaries. Even though Captain Arthur turned out to be a poor treasure hunter, he seems to have been an excellent con-man.

Siegel's hunt, which lasted only a few weeks, was an absolute farce and "Bugsy's" idea of treasure hunting by throwing hand grenades about the jungle can hardly be considered a serious search.

The only remaining question is: Was any treasure placed there at all? When Morgan became governor in Jamaica he may have sent an expedition to recover the loot he stored there although that still leaves the gold from the Spanish ships that Wafer and Davis preyed upon. Thus, it is possible the treasure is on the island yet. This argument is supported by a number of facts. First, neither David nor Wafer died rich men, implying that they never retrieved much of the wealth they accumulated over the years. And since they both robbed the seas on the western coast of Latin America, their booty could still be in that area. They would have had to store it on an island because the Spaniards ruled the coast and the pirates would not land and risk capture. The island selected would have had to be uninhabited so the group would not be noticed. The conclusion is that Cocos Island would be the perfect pirate treasure trove.

So the chance of treasure being buried on the island is fairly great. However, the chance that Cocos Island will ever release its fabled wealth to the world is probably much lower.

11

WORKING BIBLIOGRAPHY

"Assails Treasure Hunt." New York Times, 30 October 1935, p. 10.

"British Renew Hunt for Cocos Treasure." New York Times, 4 June 1935, p. 25.

"Cocos Island Gold to be Sought Again." New York Times, 22 November 1931, sec. 3, p. 6.

"Cocos Island a Place of Fabled Treasure." New York Times, 31 January 1932, sec. 5, p. 19.

"Cocos Island Treasure Hunters Report They Are Still on Job." New York Times, 24 July 1932, p. 9.

"Cocos Isle Police Squad Sends Appeal for Food." New York Times, 26 November 1935, p. 18.

"Cocos Treasure Hunters Reported Near Mutiny." New York Times, 20 September 1935, p. 5.

"Cocos Treasure Search Ends as Permit Expires." New York Times, 21 April 1935, p. 19.

"Costa Rica Gives Permit for British Treasure Hunt." New York Times, 5 April 1935, p. 4.

"Costa Rica Will Evict Cocos Treasure Hunters." New York Times, 19 February 1936, p. 10.

"Devonshire Treasure Reportedly Discovered." New York Times, 6 July 1932, p. 19.

"Engineers to Seek Cocos Island Gold." New York Times, 16 September 1934, p. 4.

"Gold Seekers Destitute." New York Times, 4 May 1936, p. 11.

"Gold Seekers Go Home." New York Times, 14 November 1934, p. 8.

"Jimenez Rescinds Order." New York Times, 21 February 1936, p. 11.

"Morgan, Sir Henry." Cyclopedia of Names. New York: Harper and Row, 1954.

Nash, Jay Robert, Bloodletters and Badmen (New York: M. Evans and Co., 1973), p. 513.

12

"President Goes Fishing and Spins Pirate Yarns." New York Times, 24
     February 1940, p. 7.

"Reports of Hardship on Cocos Isle Denied." New York Times, 25 July
     1932, p. 2.

Savell, Morton. "Cocos Island Perennial Goal of Treasure Seekers."
     Literary Digest, 14 April 1934, pp. 42-43.

"Ship Goes for Cocos Band." New York Times, 22 October 1934, p. 9.

"Treasure Discovery Denied." New York Times, 7 July 1932, p. 19.

"Treasure Hunt Ends." New York Times, 11 March 1936, p. 21.

"Treasure Hunters Held." New York Times, 14 October 1934, p. 2.

"Treasure Hunters May Go Free Today." New York Times, 29 November
     1934, p. 6.

"Treasure Hunters Offer Apology." New York Times, 15 October 1934, p.
     6.

"Treasure Hunters Tire of Wild Pig Diet." New York Times, 25 December
     1932, p. 6.

"Treasure Seekers Arrested." Literary Digest, 27 October 1934, p. 8.

"Vancouver Treasure Hunters Leave for Cocos Island." New York Times,
     22 February 1932, p. 35.

THE AXE AND FIRE MURDER OF MAJOR EVERETT S. COFRAN

by Ralph Hultin

In 1946 Germany suffered from the ravages of a war which had con-
sumed nearly all of its available resources and left it without the
manpower to replenish them to an adequate level. These conditions were
ideal for extensive black market smuggling of food, and German-American
rings flourished, particularly in Passau, located on the Danube River,
which was used as a storage center prior to distribution throughout
Germany and the surrounding countries. Major Everett S. Cofran assumed
his duties as Military Governor for this district, and quickly made it
clear he would not tolerate smuggling in his area; to that end he brought
Captain Adrian L. Wessler, military prosecutor for the Regensburg district, and his assistant, Lieutenant Stanley Rosewater, to Passau to
help him crack the smuggling ring. Early on the morning of January 7,
1946, the three men were slain in a brutal axe and fire murder, the investigation of which extended over a period of nine years and involved
American and German military and civil police in an attempt to determine
whether black marketeers or an angry American officer killed them.

The night the murder took place Rosewater slept in the major's bed,
Wessler stayed in the guest room, and Cofran went upstairs to a spare
room in the attic. All three were killed during the night when the
murderer(s) hacked the officers six to ten times in the head with an
axe from the Villa Botschafter,[1] sprinkled gasoline around the upper

---

1. In 1946 investigators believed the axe used in the crime came
from the Villa Botschafter because it was discovered in the river after
a woman pointed it out. It was later demonstrated not to be the right
one.

1

2

floor of the Villa Koller,[2] and ignited it. The autopsies indicated
Lieutenant Rosewater was the only one killed by the axe blows, but
Wessler and Cofran were still alive when the flames reached them at
approximately half-past four in the morning.[3]

Army investigators initially pursued the possibility that the officers had been killed by German "werewolves"--Nazis who refused to accept
Germany's defeat in the war--but failed to learn anything which would
substantiate this. They also questioned Cofran's peg-legged German
chauffeur with no results, and failed to learn anything by checking to
see if one or more resentful Nazis had killed Major Cofran because of
his strict administration of denazification orders. The investigators
began to get results when they learned Major Cofran and the other two
officers had been attempting to crack open a black market ring; they then
began to operate under the assumption smugglers did it and shortly uncovered a "hot lead" which led them to believe American soldiers in an
American-German black market ring had murdered the three men to prevent
their lucrative smuggling operations from being ended. The investigation
was soon made top secret in order to ensure "the direct success of the
mission," and the New York Times quoted the U.S. Army newspaper, the
Stars and Stripes, as announcing the investigators were close to bringing the case to a conclusion with the possible arrest of an American

2. The Villa Koller was the residence of Major Cofran; it was next
door to the Villa Botschafter, where Captain James M. Leech lived (he
will be referred to later).

3. Later reports stated the murders took place at two o'clock in
the morning, but these came eight years later, in 1954. Investigators
originally believed Cofran was the only one struck by an axe while the
other two were beaten with a club. All subsequent newspaper reports,
however, indicated all three men had been struck by an axe.

3

officer.[4] The case was reported as "narrowing down," although there were no official reports regarding the motive.[5] This was the last mention of the case for eight years, with no reported prosecution, nor was there even a statement concerning the results of the investigation.

In May 1954, William D. Canfield, Deputy U.S. Prosecutor for the legal department of the U.S. High Commissioner in Germany, resurrected the unsolved murder case by charging ex-Captain James M. Leech with the "axe-and-fire slaying" of the three officers. The seven-count indictment included murder, intentional manslaughter, and fatal arson, and was signed by Judge DeWitt White, who requested that Leech be extradited to stand trial in Germany.[6] Mr. Canfield believed Leech was the murderer because he had examined a "mass of evidence" which he claimed made "stranger reading than Erle Stanley Gardner."[7]

According to Canfield, Major Cofran was probably Leech's intended victim, but he didn't sleep in his own bed that night; this necessitated the killing of Wessler and Rosewater whom Leech found while searching the house for the major. The prosecutor termed the motive "personal animosity and professional jealousy"[8] because Leech's German girlfriend, who worked in the U.S. Occupation offices of Passau, was fired by Cofran; Canfield also said the Military Governor had put an end to the preferen-

---

4. "Murders in Germany Now Made Top Secret," New York Times, 17 January 1946, p. 14.

5. Ibid.

6. It is interesting to note that White was one of the Army's top investigators for the case in 1946, and that he was being mentioned as possible prosecutor when his term expired June 1, if Leech were extradited.

7. "1946 Murder of Three Officers in Germany Laid to Ohioan," New York Times, 22 May 1954, p. 1, 30.

8. "1946 Murder of Three Officers," p. 30.

4

tial treatment her father was receiving in the award of city contracts. At the same time, Leech was supposed to have been angry because Cofran was transferred to assume the position he himself had expected to get. Canfield did not accept the proposition that black market operators or embittered Nazis had killed Cofran, because he felt Cofran had been too recently transferred to the Passau district to make any enemies among the Germans.

There was other evidence contributing to Canfield's belief in Leech's guilt, among which was the fact that Leech was the only officer in the compound who could not "prove" he was elsewhere at the time the murders were committed. Three of the six men were victims, and two, "a Lieutenant in the Villa Koller and a Captain in the Villa Botschafter, had what Mr. Canfield called 'nylon-clad alibis'--German girls who were with them."[9] In Canfield's mind, however, the most damning evidence was that which seemed to indicate the crime was an "inside job." The basement door to the Villa Botschafter, usually locked, was found standing open the next morning; it was not forced, which meant it was either opened with a key or from the inside. The axe used[10] to hack the men was found in the Danube River (it was believed to have come from Leech's house). The prosecutor also said Captain Wessler had locked the door and laid a pistol on the night table next to his bed before he went to sleep. The door to his room was not forced, nor was the pistol disturbed, leading Canfield to conclude Wessler had opened the door for someone he knew and trusted. He believed Leech was incriminated beyond a doubt, and asked High Commissioner James B. Conant to extradite

---

9. *Ibid.*

10. This will be qualified later.

5

Leech to face trial in an American civil court in Germany.[11]

In response to Canfield's firmly avowed belief in Leech's guilt, Bart E. Sullivan, who had been in charge of the 1946 investigation, commented he was surprised by the prosecutor's action; he believed Leech to be innocent of the crime of which he was accused. Canfield reacted to this by charging Sullivan with "bungling." "It is my opinion," Mr. Canfield replied, "that if Sullivan were not in charge of the investigation, an arrest would have been made within forty-eight hours after the crime."[12] When Lieutenant Colonel Morton S. Jaffe, chief of special assignments of the Military Justice Branch in Europe, reviewed the case, he too was surprised there had been no trial in 1946;[13] German police simultaneously declared inexperienced Army agents "bungled" the investigation and destroyed much of the evidence.[14] The state police chief for the Passau district said German police could have found the murderer in 1946 if the Army had given them more freedom.[15,16]

The prosecutor also located a "mysterious" woman witness who had been afraid to tell her story before for fear of reprisal. She said she saw a man whom she was unable to identify come out of the Villa Koller and throw an object into the river before entering the Villa Botschaf-

---

11. The military could no longer court martial Leech because he had been discharged long before charges were filed.

12. "Army Sleuth Scored," New York Times, 1 June 1954, p. 3.

13. "Witness Reported in 3 Axe Murders," New York Times, 23 May 1954, p. 26.

14. Ibid.

15. "House of Axe Murders Visited," New York Times, 29 May 1954, p. 11.

16. Defense Attorney Howard Everett regarded these statements by the Germans as attempts to blacken the U.S. name because they wanted Americans out of Germany.

6

ter.[17] The axe was recovered near the spot she pointed out.

James Leech never heard anything from the officials about the re-
opened investigation; he first learned of it when reporters came to
question him concerning the case. Reporters described him as "more
puzzled than disturbed" after they discussed the case with him. He
admitted he had been one of the suspects in 1946 and was held in custody
for four months, two of those under observation in the psychiatric ward
of a hospital. "Nothing happened in the case," he affirmed, "and since
my time overseas was up and they sent me home, I thought the matter was
closed."[18] When asked what he planned to do, Mr. Leech replied: "You
can see that I'm not running away."[19] Later, in a statement released by
Howard Everett, a Lima, Ohio (Leech's hometown) attorney who volunteered
to help him, the ex-Army captain stated very simply, "I don't know who
killed them, but I didn't kill them." He also mentioned he had just met
Wessler and Rosewater the day they were murdered.

It was obvious the Army believed Mr. Leech was innocent, since
after giving him a polygraph test, sodium pentathol, and placing him
under custody for four months, they transferred him to another unit and
placed him in command until his time was up and then gave him an honorable discharge. He was recalled to active duty in 1950 and served for
two more years after which he received a second honorable discharge.
Had they wished, the Army could have prosecuted him in 1946 or 1950; by
failing to do so they demonstrated their belief in his innocence.

Howard Everett, Mr. Leech's defense attorney, also believed his

-----

17. "Witness Reported in 3 Axe Murders," New York Times, 23 May
1954, p. 26.

18. "Leech is Puzzled," New York Times, 22 May 1954, p. 1, 30.

19. Ibid.

7

client was innocent of the murder because he talked to the Army prose-

cutor from 1946 and "he believed that Leech was innocent. They proved

he was innocent."[20] Mr. Everett declared without reservation Mr. Leech

was not the type of person to be jealous of Major Cofran for receiving

a job he might have desired, nor was he the type to become angry enough

to kill his superior if he had a girlfriend who was fired. He even went

so far as to say:

> He was interested in all kinds of community work.
> Worked with the Boy Scouts . . . he studied all the
> Indian lore in this particular part of the country.
> He had painted pictures of all the Indian chiefs that
> lived in this part of Ohio . . . he didn't do it; Jim
> wasn't the type--I've known him all my life . . . he
> was always interested in history, and folklore, and
> Indian lore, and Boy Scouting, fishing and boating,
> and all that kind of stuff. He was not the type to
> kill a person.[21]

Although Major Cofran had only recently been transferred to Passau before

he was killed, Everett felt there was sufficient time for him to convince

black market operators he was going to do everything within his power to

destroy their smuggling ring, thus forcing them to kill him quickly. The

attorney remembered Cofran's making a speech to the people of Passau to

the effect that he was going to put a sudden halt to the smuggling.[22]

The Ohio attorney also placed little credence in the testimony of

the German prostitutes who defended the other officers; he responded to

a statement regarding Leech's lack of an "alibi" by saying: "What you

mean is that he was the only one that didn't have a German girl with

---

20. Information received in a telephone call to Attorney Howard
Everett of Lima, Ohio, by the author, 7 November 1973.

21. Information in a telephone call to Attorney Howard Everett of
Lima by the author, 7 November 1973.

22. Information received in a telephone call to Howard Everett by
the author, 19 November 1973.

8

him!"[23] Not only did he find this evidence unsatisfactory, but he
learned also that the axe recovered from the river was not the axe used
in the murder. When it was found, the Army investigator took the axe
and checked to see if it would fit into the wounds in the victims' heads,
and it wouldn't,[24] thus determining positively that it was not the murder
weapon. Mr. Everett believed the woman who said she saw it thrown into
the river may have been lying in order to divert suspicion away from
black market operators with whom she was allied, either by choice or by
coercion.[25] He had further grounds for believing in Leech's innocence
after learning from a German lawyer that it was the "modus operandi" of
German gangsters to kill someone and set the building they were in afire,
much the same as it was standard for American gangsters in the 1920s to
machine gun their victims.

While this murder case is far too confusing to make any absolute
statements about the murderer(s), it is easier to believe black market
operators murdered the three officers than to believe James Leech did.
There are too many unanswered questions, too many holes, too much con-
jecture, and not enough solid evidence to indicate he did it. If Leech
did it for reasons of "personal animosity and professional jealousy,"
he would have been foolish to do it the one night two visitors were
staying with Major Cofran. He had opportunities to kill Cofran before;
he should have done it then, or after the two visitors left Cofran's
quarters. Everett's testimony on Leech's character makes Canfield's
suppositions even less credible, and the fact that he didn't have a girl

---

23. Ibid.

24. Ibid.

25. Ibid.

9

with him lends credence to this. In addition, it seems unlikely that one man could have killed the other three without awakening them, especially when it was reported in 1946 that a Major Hugo Hessen escaped when he heard the noise upstairs. The pistol in Wessler's room may have been placed on the night stand to make it appear as if he had opened the door for someone he trusted.

If it is remembered that the German black market operators would be professionals and dangerous, it is not too difficult to explain most of the questions that arise in believing they committed the crime. It would be very convenient for them if all three officers committed to cracking the smuggling ring were killed, removing the greatest obstacle to their continued success. It is not unlikely one or more of the girls and/or Americans could have been allied with them and could have provided keys or opened the doors to the two houses from the inside. Thus the murderer(s) could have had entry into Cofran's house as well as Leech's (to act as a decoy) without breaking in. It is also possible the three men were drugged to prevent them from awakening,[26] which would explain how three men could be killed without waking up. It would also have been foolish for Leech to stop on the lawn where everybody could see him, throw an object in the river in view of anybody nearby, and then conspicuously enter the basement of his house without locking the door behind him. What makes this story even more believable is the fact that the axe planted in the river was not the murder weapon; that axe was obviously a decoy.

Mr. Everett believed there was a good reason the High Commission

---

26. The German couple that tended the villa believed they'd been drugged so they slept through the crime. ("Witness Reported in 3 Axe Murders," p. 26.)

10

supported Canfield's version; he realized they were in the process of folding up and wanted to keep their nice lucrative jobs. "They wanted to drag up anything they could to hold it open," he averred. "Those buzzards were not for political jobs . . . all they wanted to do was perpetuate themselves in office."[27] That would also explain why near the end of the case Canfield called on Congress to investigate what he called "an attempt to bring down a curtain of silence"[28] on the investigation. What better way to attract attention and insure the continued existence of the High Commission than to involve Congress?

The Justice Department rightly concluded there was insufficient evidence to extradite Leech; however, even if they had said there was enough evidence the High Commission lacked the jurisdiction to extradite him.[29] The crime was committed under the Army's jurisdiction because Leech was in America, and the High Commission did not yet exist when he was in Germany. American civil courts could not try Leech because the crime was committed in Germany while he was in the Army. Thus there was no court in the world which could try Leech unless he went back into the Army, and he never had a chance to do that--he was killed in an explosion at an oil refinery in 1956 while welding an oil-filled boiler.

The Major Everett S. Cofran murder case once again reached an unsatisfying conclusion as the High Commission was dissolved in April, 1955, with no prosecution, and no conviction, other than what Everett

27. Information in a telephone call to Attorney Howard Everett of Lima by the author, 7 November 1973.

28. "Congress Inquiry Urged," New York Times, 10 June 1954, p. 10.

29. George T. Davis, a San Francisco lawyer in Germany who pretended to be hired by Leech as "legal observer," made this announcement to the press, as well as did Everett. ("Extradition Off in Axe Murders," New York Times, 24 May 1954, p. 5.)

11

called a "newspaper conviction" of Leech. The decision of choosing the
guilty party remains up to the judgment of the reader and his interpre-
tation of the facts.

12

WORKING BIBLIOGRAPHY

"Army Sleuth Scored." New York Times, 1 June 1954, p. 3.

"Asks Extradition Ruling." New York Times, 19 June 1954, p. 3.

"Congress Inquiry Urged." New York Times, 10 June 1954, p. 10.

"Extradition Off in Axe Murders." New York Times, 24 May 1954, p. 5.

"Extradition Procedure." New York Times, 22 May 1954, p. 30.

"Figure in Slaying Dies in Ohio of Burn." New York Times, 4 March 1956, p. 78.

"GI's at Murder Site Told to Carry Arms." New York Times, 14 January 1946, p. 4.

"GI's Linked to Killing." New York Times, 15 January 1946, p. 16.

"House of Axe Murders Visited." New York Times, 29 May 1954, p. 11.

Information received in a phone call by the author to Howard Everett, a Lima, Ohio attorney, 7 November 1973.

Information received in a phone call by the author to Howard Everett, a Lima, Ohio attorney, 19 November 1973.

"Leech Denies Charges." New York Times, 23 May 1954, p. 26.

"Leech is Puzzled." New York Times, 22 May 1954, p. 30.

"Murders in Germany Now Made Top Secret." New York Times, 17 January 1946, p. 14.

"Murders in the Villa Koller." Newsweek, 31 May 1954, p. 40.

"1946 Murder of Three Officers Laid to Ohioan." New York Times, 22 May 1954, p. 1, 30.

"Obituary." Time, 19 March 1956, p. 107.

"Officers' Murder Recalls Holohan." New York Times, 22 May 1954, p. 30.

"Slayer of 3 Officers Hunted in Germany." New York Times, 13 January 1946, p. 23.

"3 U.S. Officers Die in German Lodgings." New York Times, 12 January 1946, p. 6.

13

"U.S. Closes Inquiry on German Slaying." New York Times, 27 April
     1955, p. 6.

"U.S. Pushes Leech Case." New York Times, 31 May 1954, p. 6.

"Witness Reported in 3 Axe Murders." New York Times, 23 May 1954,
     p. 26.

THE PROCESS

GUIDELINES FOR RESEARCHING
AND WRITING ABOUT A NEWSPAPER CASE

Researching popular topics through contemporary newspapers presents its own unique problems (and rewards). Teachers need to be especially aware of two of these problems. The first is that students are in complete command of their topic. No one else in the school (probably even the country) has more information than they do. In a sense, they will become the world's expert on a piece of historical minutia. This is as it should be, but at times it is difficult to provide specific help in the same way one could if the topic were on, say, *Moby Dick*. Still, most students will be able to handle the research on their own. Just warn them that newspapers often cover a story only when it's "hot." Later stories may fill in missing pieces, or students may find that details initially considered important fade as more bizarre elements enter the case.

The second unique aspect of this assignment is that these kinds of topics, although encased in a chronological format, are not neatly organized like a literary assignment. There are false leads, surprising revelations, characters who appear and disappear—in short, it is a real research problem rather than a manufactured topic. It is probably best to tell students to wade through it the first time as though the case were a Faulkner novel, and then begin to assimilate the important material into a streamlined account. The process of understanding the topic, choosing salient facts, selecting striking quotations, and putting everything in readable form is what writing a research paper is all about. Footnotes and bibliography, although important, are all mechanical items that come during the final writing.

LIBRARY RESEARCH EXERCISES

For many students a library can be a scary place. All those books, people working so quietly—everybody seems to know what they're doing and they all look so confident. Most students have been to the library before and can use the card catalog, and with a little luck they can find the book they're after (if it hasn't been lost or stolen or checked out by a faculty member for the past two years). But it's a frustrating experience because they know there's material there that would help them with a paper if only they could stumble across it. When it comes to indexes and micromaterials the situation is often frightening because most students have never used these and perhaps don't know they exist. I have found that a library tour which concentrates almost exclusively on these items is worth the time. Even the process of physically putting a reel of microfilm on the machine is not too mundane a maneuver; students can see how to adjust the focus and then correctly reshelve the material. College librarians seem eager to help with this, and they become "willing accomplices" when students investigate their cases.

At the conclusion of the tour I pass out a brief research exercise sheet designed to force students into using the indexes and microfilm machines that have just been examined. The three items should average out to a page and a half and take about forty-five minutes to complete.

1. What happened on the day you were born? or *Write a brief paragraph on what happened in the world on this date in the year* _____. (Deal especially with "curiosities," the sociology of the times, and advertisements.)

These questions force students to actually put a reel of the New York Times on a microfilm machine and use it. When writing about the day of their birth, students should touch on world news, sports, movies playing at the time, and want ads. Currently I use the latter question, giving each student a different year in the nineteenth century. Then, by using the current month and day, I ask for a brief paragraph on the "temper of the times." Ask them to explain what the quality of life was like on, say, September 4, 1883. Impress upon them to stay away from floods, world news, etc., but instead concentrate on the "passions" and "oddities" of the day. How did people live? What did they wear? What strange news stories appeared? Most students find this fascinating and the results are often interesting to read.

Sample response

On January 19, 1882, there seemed to be as many disasters in the news as there are today. There were quite a few fires, ship wrecks, murders, and a freight train was demolished while "running over 30 miles an hour."

Opera houses were popular entertainment in the North, as were "lynching parties" in the South. For 25¢ one could use tobogan trails or play polo, and for $1.50 one could have an orchestra seat at Augustin Daly's Broadway comedy Railroad of Love. Curling, a game played on ice with large rounded stones, and playing the zither, a flat stringed instrument, were both popular pastimes. A tour in the tropical seas was $5 a day on Atlas Lines' "comfortable passenger steamers."

On this day the New York Times offered two positions for females: one as a laundress and the other as a chambermaid. More jobs were advertised for men, but they didn't show any improvement—mostly butlers and office boys. Immigrants offered their services as cooks, governesses, nurses, coachmen, and grooms. Most applicants were not so much interested in salary as in a good home. Religion, race, and sobriety were always mentioned in ads.

Obituaries listed ten children who died at about the age of one year. There were three suicides, one because of "unrequited love." Duffy's Pure Malt Whiskey claimed it could cure the common cold, while Bromo Effervescent Caffeine simply stated it "cures all."

The article I found the most fascinating was entitled "Breaking Stone for a Kiss." The story concerned a man arrested for kissing a strange woman on the cheek. He was charged with assault and sentenced to six months at hard labor.

Betsy Banham

2. Write a brief account of the Harvard/Yale game in the year _____. (How the game was played, the cheers, the dress styles, etc.)

This requires students to use the New York Times Index for the first time. It works well using any year since the 1880s. Ask students to include the score, the heroes, how the game of football was played at that time and what people wore. (This was a social event as much as anything else and often received front page coverage.) In a few of the years no game was played, but there is usually an explanation given and this, or an alternate game, can substitute. Most students will be surprised at how much football has changed and how descriptive the accounts are, e.g., "Haskell was laid out with an unlucky blow in the face, from which blood streamed." Team cheers are often quoted and they also prove interesting. (My favorite is "breck-akek-kek, co-ax, co-ax! whoo-up, whoo-up, paraballo '92'.")

Sample response

Harvard and Yale did not play each other from 1894 to 1896, so I chose the Yale/Carlisle game that was played on October 25, 1896. Yale was a football power and Carlisle was a team with good size but without much knowledge of the game. Yale was expected to run away with the contest but didn't.

According to the New York Times account of the game, Carlisle outplayed Yale but was the victim of a "wrong decision" on the part of referee W. O. Hickcock. In the second half, with Yale leading 12–6, Carlisle running back Seneca broke a few tackles and scampered 37 yards for a touchdown. The 5,000 spectators cheered wildly (they were pro-Carlisle) and "men waved their hats in the air, pretty girls clapped their hands and above the din could be heard the shrill Indian cry of "hi, hi, Carlisle, hi, hi!" But their joy was short-lived as Hickcock called the play back because he thought Yale had stopped Seneca near the line of scrimmage. An argument erupted and Carlisle threatened to walk off the field if the TD didn't count. The referee persisted and the game eventually continued after some heated discussion. Yale won, but the real winners were Carlisle. After the game the fans rushed the field, hoisted the Carlisle players on their shoulders and carried them off amid a wave of cheering.

Chris Williams

3. Pick one movie made in the year _____ and tell what the critics thought about it. (Try to pick a title that sounds particularly corny.)

The third item is designed to show students how to use the *Readers' Guide to Periodical Literature* and then look up a magazine article from it. I begin with the year 1930, and by assigning different years I ask students to select a movie that sounds unusual and particularly corny (*Bonzo Goes to College*, *Superman in the Volcano*, *Gog*). I then ask for a synopsis of one or two magazines' reviews of the film. In order to complete this assignment students must use the *Readers' Guide*, the library's circular file of catalogued periodicals, and magazine articles in a bound volume or on microfilm.

Sample response

Time magazine described the 1946 film *Smoky* as "the story of a long, beautiful, rather intense friendship between Fred MacMurray and a horse." (Nowadays, such a description would lead to just one conclusion—rated X.) Actually, *Newsweek* called *Smoky* "a natural for youngsters and horse lovers. . . it makes a pleasant evening even for the nonequestrian moviegoer." In the film, Smoky, who has the distinction of playing both himself and the title role, is a beautiful black stallion who is adored by everyone—everyone, that is, except the villain (Bruce Cabot). There's the usual boy/girl thing between MacMurray and Anne Baxter, but it never really gets very far and *Time* stated that "the important relationship is between Cowpuncher MacMurray and stallion." Burl Ives made his film debut here and sang "Streets of Laredo," "Down in the Valley," and "Blue Tail Fly." Both *Time* and *Newsweek* treated the new film enthusiastically, perhaps because the crux of the story was about a horse—a nice shiny black horse who doesn't smoke, drink or watch television. As *Newsweek* said, "the human beings do a nice job, but Smoky steals the show."

Bill Calaman

This general format can be used for assignments in *Book Review Digest*, *Education Index*, *Essay and General Literature Index*, and *PMLA Bibliographies*, but they are not as interesting nor are they really needed for researching murder cases. At a different point in the course I do ask students to look up one issue of *Popular Mechanics* (dating from 1902) and report on one of the more bizarre inventions of the day. These reports on electric chairs to cure seasickness, spikes to keep boys off the rears of cars, and automatic music page turners are usually fascinating. By this time students are quite familiar with the library's reference section and are able to begin research papers that use these kinds of resources.

PREPARATION AND RESEARCH

Gaining Perspective

Now that students have had some research experience in the library, I am ready to introduce the project and assign the topics. For the most part I just shuffle the case cards and deal them out, but occasionally I take requests or attempt to match special cases to certain students. At the outset of the course I ask each student to indicate personal interests (sports, crime, Indians, historical era, etc.) as well as home town and college major. Sometimes I am able to assign a student a home town case, or one that fits a specific interest, but this is rather rare.

Upon receiving their cards, the students begin to immerse themselves in the time period. I tell them to "think 1878," for example, and they must write a brief page on what life was like in their year. What concerned people? What did they wear? Who was important? What entertainment existed? (This is like question one in the previous assignment but now students will probably do a better job.) In many instances, this information can be used in the introduction to the paper, especially if the murder case reflects dated mores or customs of the era. In the Frank T. Young case, the murder occurs in a Hanson Cab, but the girl with this topic had no idea what a Hanson Cab was so she had to look it up before she could continue her paper. Red Cassidy's murder in 1929 seems right out of the movies, and it was necessary for the student to read books on the gangland period to put it into perspective. This background research sets the scene for detailed investigation later. A brief perusal of scattered newspapers during that year usually suffices, but enterprising students will find books of popular history to read. (About a week into their research, I ask them who the President was during the period they are researching. Some are chagrined when they don't know.)

Next, students must ascertain the general layout and circumstances of their cases as best they can by using the *New York Times Index*. I ask them not to go to the papers themselves, but to scan the headings in the *Index* and fill in certain information on a "research paper fact sheet" (see sample). Item one establishes the dates a case begins and ends, essential in ascertaining the scope of a case. Most of the cases continue for a period of years, and because of frequent changes in the *Index*'s format, it is easy to

Name: _____

Research Paper Fact Sheet

Working Title of Paper:

1. Period of time encompassed by topic. (Give exact date of first
    story and the year and month of conclusion.)

2. Categories under which topic is indexed.

3. Periodical Sources. (List articles in magazines, books, and all
    newspaper editorials on case.)

4. Locale where events took place. (Use an atlas if needed--try to
    find a local map if possible.)

5. People involved. (List major figures in case--victim, killer,
    detectives, etc.)

6. The amount of material on my topic is A) enormous B) very great
    C) adequate D) somewhat less than adequate E) meager.

miss items without careful research. (In the middle nineteenth century a number of years appear in the same *Index*; in the 1920s each year is divided into six-month periods; and in the 1930s the *Index* is in two volumes alphabetically divided.) The headings usually give students an idea of what the case is all about and when the topic ends, but once into the case, some are surprised to discover that an article may appear many years later.

Item two alerts students to the headings under which their topic is indexed. Major headings often change as the case progresses; early years are subject oriented under "Editorials," "Political," "War," and "Miscellaneous."

Item three requires a list of periodical sources, and sends students to the *Readers' Guide to Periodical Literature* (or to *Poole's Index* if the case is before 1890). About a fourth of the topics listed at the end of this book are the subject of magazine articles or are cited in books. (Any case that resulted in a trial of some kind has a good chance of being reported in magazines, if only by a short notice.) Some students, willing to settle for newspaper articles alone, become easily discouraged when trying to use the archaic format in *Poole's Index* (which lists magazine articles from 1802–1906). They should be encouraged to use this and other references, and warned to check as far as ten years beyond their case's conclusion for material. Students are also asked to note any editorials on their case, as they are must reading.

Usually the major headings (e.g., "murder") are all that are needed here, but sometimes articles are cited by key names in the case. *The International Index to Periodicals* (beginning in 1907 but changing in 1965 to the *Social Science and Humanities Index*) is a helpful tool. Other reference books that may include material and are worth checking are *Index to Legal Periodicals* and *Psychoanalysis, Psychiatry, and Law*. Later, students may need to use *A Dictionary of the Underworld* by Eric Partridge, the *Encyclopedia of Crimes and Criminals*, and the *Dictionary of Criminology* to look up special terms. The remaining items on the fact sheet are self-explanatory. After students hand this in, class discussion about their cases usually generates enthusiasm for getting started, and it is sometimes difficult to keep students from moving ahead before they are ready.

Research with the Accent on the Last Syllable

Before students can begin reading and notetaking, they must decide what they will read. I ask them to go back to the *New York Times Index* and select the stories they plan to read. Because nearly every case has a great deal of material, it is necessary for students to screen the articles carefully. Some students do this better than others, of course, but rough guidelines can be employed. If a head reads "Police Continue Search for Killer," it can be assumed that nothing new will be revealed and the article is hardly worth reading. Trials drag on, and something like "Coroner Testifies Today" can probably be left out. Appeals, jury selection, stays of execution—any item that doesn't indicate in the headline that the case is developing significantly (especially retrials with predictable outcomes) can usually be deleted. But there are no hard and fast rules. The William McClintock murder requires a close reading of something like sixty articles—almost the entire case—while the Sir Roger Charles Tichborne fiasco has over 200 stories, but only about thirty-five key items need to be read. As a general rule, the more the person reads the better off he or she is and the greater the chances for a good paper. But students tell me they take other classes besides mine (I sometimes forget that) and must fit their research into available time. When students become lost because they have selected too few articles, they can always backtrack and pick up missed stories.

As the students screen their articles, they are required to copy the essential information for finding them. (I suggest that each student buy a spiral notebook to keep this and other research material in. The chronological nature of the cases lends itself to the notebook, or note cards, procedure.) A typical *Index* entry under "Murders" might be: "Logan, (Mrs.) M; body found; Mrs. L. B. Judson admits burying it; she and husband arraigned, Los Angeles, D 23, 15:7." Among other things, students learn the story is in the *New York Times* of December 23 (they should also jot down the year—1944 in this case); I tell them to forget the column number (the last figure) because they will quickly spot the case on the page. And I warn them to be very careful to get the page number correct (page 15 in this sample). Almost every student will notice mistakes between dates and page numbers from the *New York Times Index* and the papers themselves, and this proves exasperating enough without copying the pages incorrectly to begin with. Students will encounter juicy sounding stories listed in the *Index* that simply don't exist; or they will find them on the wrong pages; or they will stumble across them in papers printed a month later along with stories that were never indexed. It is also important to be on the lookout for mistakes in the day to day unraveling of a case. Names will be spelled several ways, facts will be reversed, people shot in opening stories turn out to be hanged in later accounts. (Notice content footnotes in the sample cases.) In short, there are as many mistakes in nineteenth century papers as there are in news stories today. This forces students to be careful researchers—one of the project goals. *And most important of all, I warn students, upon threat of death or failure, not to write in the* Index. The assigned students are usually the only ones dealing with that case in the history of the school, so tell them any underlined items are like leaving fingerprints.

The first week of this project is a key period because, in a sense, students are constructing their bibliographies. Care must be taken that all pages of any given story are included and that the important sources are recorded for future reading. I request a minimum of twenty-five sources, but thirty is better, and some run to forty or more. The key is that they include the necessary stories to construct a ten to twelve page paper.

Words of Caution

As students begin reading and taking notes, the key item to stress is that they be as accurate as possible. News stories in papers from earlier periods read far differently than modern accounts. It seems no one ever died without a reporter hovering near to record a melodramatic statement, and every event is "the most dastardly crime ever perpetrated in this fair city." Autopsies are reprinted, reporters have no qualms about accusing suspects, and editors always seem incensed about justice (or the lack of it). Racism is blatant, violence is quick, and sex is only hinted at. Students will be dumbstruck over some of the attitudes, and the "language" of the stories makes for some interesting class discussions. In a sense, more is told in these stories, but the chronological sequence of events is sometimes inaccurate in order to concentrate on the sensational material. Caution students to be skeptical, read between the lines, and actually research words they don't understand. Sex crimes are a case in point, for the crime is often explained in coded terms. (When it is reported that an "outrage" was committed, it means the girl was raped.) Psychiatrists are called "alienists," the Tombs is the name

for the New York City detention center, "arsenic eating" was the practice of swallowing arsenic to impart a light complexion for cosmetic purposes, "white slavers" seem to lurk everywhere—it was the best of times, the worst of times. *All stories need to be taken with a grain of salt* and all sources evaluated in the same way modern scholars investigate conclusions arrived at by earlier researchers.

Remind students that important details, such as physical descriptions, are often given when a story breaks, but are never repeated. On the other hand, newspapers will give vast coverage to items that ultimately are of little importance simply because there is nothing else to report. (In the Anna Aumuller case, abundant space was devoted to stories about the kind of rock found with the body, a dead-end clue that was never mentioned again after an arrest was made.) In a sense, the student must provide an exact, step-by-step reconstruction of what happened, even filling in gaps with logical hypotheses if needed.

If a case goes to trial, the coverage tends to be daily, with long stretches of dialogue that simply lay the groundwork for future evidence. In these cases, students can scan the material very quickly. In fact, there are times when twenty stories can be reduced to a single line, such as: "After a long trial Albert Fish was convicted and sentenced to death."

A better method of dealing with trial material is to tell students to take courtroom testimony and use it elsewhere in the paper. During the trial, facts about the crime itself will come out that can be used in the introduction to the paper. Thus, rather than repeat the case or use the trial as the focal point, it is often possible to treat the trial as a single source of information. (This is especially true where biographical material on the victim or murderer is brought out.)

At the same time students are researching indexed stories or articles, they should be alert for material that was never cited, especially letters-to-the-editor. Cases that capture public attention often bring community reactions which range from the violent to the bizarre, and sometimes they reveal attitudes not reflected in news stories themselves. A quick glance at editorial pages is worth the effort, and a keen eye almost always results in a find of uncataloged material. (The *New York Times* indexing for the early years is particularly "incomplete.")

Finally, it is important to warn students never to assume their case is over. People rarely stay in prison for life, or they make news while in prison, or at times they escape from prison. I ask that everyone go at least five years beyond the "last" story in the *New York Times Index* to be sure nothing new occurs that should be reported, and sometimes even that is not far enough. Magazine articles appear that recap the case and add further information some twenty years later, while unsolved cases are mentioned in the news every time a similar crime takes place. Harry Thaw, who killed Stanford White in 1906, was later convicted of assaulting a young boy and finally died in 1947, at which time the papers reviewed his life. It is worth remembering, too, that any event touching on Patty Hearst will make news the rest of her life.

This may be the point at which the traditional cautions about plagiarism should be mentioned. Tell students you don't want to read the old newspaper stories, but want to see their account—written in a modern style—of what happened. Occasionally I do receive research papers taken word for word from the newspapers, but the "style" shows every time. When a boxer is "thrown against the hempen strands," or a man "succumbed to a wound by his unregenerated cohort," it's pretty obvious that the student didn't write it. Most people will be forced to reshape the material because it is so badly written in the newspapers or the language is so out of date. Those rare papers that are plagiarized usually have tense and language problems so pronounced that they fail on the basis of style alone. (A preliminary check of any rough draft material, followed, if necessary, by a mild inquiry, is usually enough to deter this practice.)

Alternate Sources

In the course of five years I have had freshman students do some amazing pieces of research, including visiting the scenes of crimes, writing descendants in the cases for information, checking trial transcripts in law libraries, and calling people once involved in the story. (In one instance I was queried by the FBI because a student tried to check out his case through an agent at the Washington office; they thought perhaps I knew something about a 1939 kidnapping that was still open on their records.) Early in the research process, I distribute a suggested format for a letter requesting information (see sample). I have found that about ten percent of any given class are able to take advantage of it.

For the most part, however, students stick to college library resources. Yet even here more is available than just the *New York Times*. I now require students to find stories in other papers and compare the accounts to decide on the accuracy of certain points. Although the *Times* is the only paper with an index to stories, it is quite easy to check exact days in other papers when a particular case is "hot." The *Philadelphia Inquirer, Chicago Tribune, New Orleans Times Picayune, Los Angeles Times, St. Louis Post Dispatch,* and many local papers all printed before the age of wire services will have revealing stories containing different information. If the library carries *Frank Leslie's Illustrated Newspaper* (1855–1922), this will give much more sensationalized accounts of cases than the *New York Times*, and students will find interesting material here. I encourage students to write letters to small town editors where a case occurred, and many times the college library can locate obscure material through inter-library loan. The student working on the 1922 Daniel Kaber murder, for instance, was sent a complete file of all the stories from the *Cleveland Plain Dealer*, while the editor of the *Hartford Courant* provided valuable assistance to a girl investigating the 1878 Mary Stannard Case. (One item was a copy of a poem that circulated at the time which concludes: "Now all young ladies a warning take/Whether you're great or small/If you would not like to be cut in pieces/And pickled in alcohol.") These kinds of exercises not only result in better student papers, but make freshmen feel they are really involved in original research.

WRITING THE PAPER

The initial time spent on research and notetaking will vary according to the student, the case involved, and the procedure used. If the student has a particularly complicated case, or it extends for a number of years, it can take as long as two weeks just to assimilate all the materials and choose what will be read. For the average student, however, one week is enough to compile a tentative list of news articles and periodical sources to be read. (Usually the list has to be expanded once the reading is underway.)

As soon as the reading is begun students probably need two to three weeks (again depending on their case) to cover all the materials, take notes, and perhaps construct a rough draft. During the period students are reading the microfilmed copies of the *New York Times* and other papers, class time will probably be spent on bibliographical format. Footnoting and footnote form are important considerations, and sample newspaper footnotes can be gone over in class. The footnotes on the papers included here generally follow the MLA format, but there are so many variations in form I hesitate to advance a definitive style. Any standard research guide works, and I leave it to teachers to decide among MLA, Turabian, Campbell, etc.

Introductions

Although a variety of introductions can be used, the typical or standard introduction for a paper of this kind is one that follows the old newspaper dictate of who, what, when, where. Because most of the research papers will follow a chronological approach, it is easy for students to begin with the first date and then explain the circumstances of the case: "On January 23, 1879, the body of Diane Gott was discovered in an abandoned house on the outskirts of Toledo, Ohio." This simple opening sentence is enough to explain the case's background and also whet the reader's appetite. This is the type of introduction used in the sample paper on Hans Schmidt and is the easiest to construct.

But even this kind of opening can be improved upon by most students with the addition of a sentence or two at the end of the introduction that puts the case into larger perspective or hints at how it will all end. The paper on Jacob Rosenzweig, for instance, has an introduction that begins with the girl's death but then moves quickly into the problem of abortion in the nineteenth century. The introductions to the papers on Laura Fair and William Kemmler both have a kind of esthetic distance to them, evoked through the use of a quotation in the last line of the introduction. Perhaps the best kind of introduction is one which deals entirely with general background, the milieu, the temper of the times. The Major Cofran paper begins by explaining the state of postwar Germany; the Red Cassidy introduction sketches the era of Prohibition; the paper on the Bannock War first reviews previous Indian conflicts. This kind of introduction tends to be much smoother than just a terse recital of the facts.

Instructors might wish to pass out copies of newsstand detective magazines as samples of how cases can be introduced. They tend to be overly dramatic (even somewhat laughable for sophisticated readers), but Professor Gene Collier of East

---

```
Name
Address
City, State


Dear _____


     As a term paper assignment in one of my college courses
I am researching the _____ murder which occurred
on _____.  To date I have read all of the accounts
of this case in the New York Times and am attempting to find
other sources that might be available.


     I would like to inquire if you might have material about
this subject or opinions on the case that might not generally
be known.  Because your paper once reported these events (or
because your family was once connected with some of these
events) I thought I would write you for information.  Any
information you could supply would be greatly appreciated.


                              Sincerely,


                              Name
                              Address
                              City, State
```

Central University in Oklahoma finds that these openings show "pizzazz and sparkle . . . and reassure the student writer that he can cause the reader to want more." At times students must be cautioned to "ease up" on their introductions and even tone down the material. Otherwise the result ends up like the following introduction I received a few years ago: "On October 14, 1911, the future of Avis Linnell was drastically changed. There was to be no future for she died in her room."

The Search for Good Quotations

Quotations can make or break a paper, so by the second week I ask students to hand in two quotations they plan to use in their final report. These are read in class and commented on, and students soon get an idea of what works and what doesn't. Anything in the nature of an opinion, theory, or conclusion by the police or the newspaper should be considered as a possible quotation, and a statement that reflects the mores or attitudes of the period is a must. Quotations that act as a brief summary of events, relate important pieces of information, give the "flavor" of the situation, are dramatic, racist, ironic or satiric, or are simply so stunning that the student marvels to himself, "I don't believe anyone would say that!" should be considered. I think many of the papers in this book exhibit good choices of quotations, but here are a few that other students have used:

> "There were many who fancied that the murder was the work of negroes, and this fancy was based upon the rumor that Mrs. Hull had been outraged before she was murdered." (Jane Hull Case, 1879)

> Mrs. Hull was buried on Saturday, June 14, 1879. Throngs of people gathered outside the house and "some of them stuck so close it was evident they would consider it an honor if the hearse had run over them." Even a few days after the burial children would come to stare at the house, yet "police made no effort to drive them away, but let them drink their fill of sensation in such little drops as they could get." (Jane Hull Case, 1879)

> "The fact that so much unnecessary violence had been used, evidently after the girl's life had been ended by the cut across the throat, suggested to many that a negro, brutal always to the last degree in such cases, was the perpetrator of the crime." (Rahway Mystery, 1887)

Class time is also spent on explaining how quotations should be used in the papers. Quotations within quotations, ellipsis marks, brackets, and punctuation marks are studied through the use of a handbook, and I urge students to replace "said" with terms such as "remarked, exclaimed, replied, declared, reported," etc. Almost every quotation needs to be worked on in some way and *sic* is used much more often with this project than in more formal papers. Because of the narrative aspect of these kinds of papers, I suggest to students that they employ their own words in the middle of quotations.

> "The plain fact is that there was no excuse whatsoever for the brutality of the police," reported a *New York Times* editorial. "If there were a spark of decency or self-respect in the minds of the police commissioners, the offenders would be sharply pursued and severely disciplined."

> "The life of one white man is worth more," stated Miss Meeker, "than all the Indians from the beginning of their creation."

These forms make the papers more readable and add a slightly creative aspect.

Further admonitions might include the warning that extremely long quotations should be avoided (people seldom read them), and that it is not a good idea to use back-to-back quotations or a long series of quotations interspersed with the author's words. A rough guideline I use is that quotations should average no more than two per page, with only two long, indented quotations in the paper.

Putting the Paper Together

One of the major advantages of these kinds of topics for beginning writers is that an organizational framework is built in; events, for the most part, proceed chronologically. Still, many of these cases are confusing, and students should be cautioned that all items must be made clear to the reader. Time jumps from one event to another need to be pointed out, and dates (including the year) should be mentioned throughout the paper. Sentences such as the following can be employed:

> "Two months later, on December 17, 1899, the case was reopened . . . . "
> "It was not until the spring of 1900 that the suspect was apprehended."
> "After nearly a year of appeals, Smith was executed on February 23, 1901."

These devices aid the reader with the sequence of events and retain the narrative aspect of the case.

Whenever possible, a person's title, or relationship to the case, should be cited to help readers identify the personalities involved. Most of the topics have a myriad of people coming and going throughout the narrative, so to make a key figure stand out (as well as to avoid repetitiveness) it is better to refer to Mr. Smith one time, the grocer another, and then call him "the suspect" in the following line.

Also, witnesses tend to repeat the same facts in newspaper accounts, and it is best if students pick just one person's story to recount rather than report essentially the same testimony from several people. I further urge students to "personalize" their papers whenever possible by including physical descriptions of people and the locale.

> On a winter afternoon in 1917, pretty eighteen-year-old Beth Pomerantz left her Pittsburgh, Pennsylvania home saying she was going to a repair shop a few blocks away to have her skates sharpened. The neighborhood near her house was frequented by many retired men who in their youth had worked in the grimy steel mills on the outskirts of the city.

Many times these details do not appear until much later in the story (often during the trial), but they can be easily incorporated in earlier parts of the paper. As mentioned before, trial material, if there is a trial, tends to be long and somewhat dry. At times whole accounts can be skimmed, especially if the information is predictable. Simply because there is more of it than other kinds of news should not seduce the student into using it in a wholesale manner.

What to Document

The decision of what to footnote is a constant problem in this and other kinds of papers. Helping students distinguish what is "general information" is something that is seldom clear until graduate school I'm afraid, but again a rough guideline can be employed. As a rule anything that is constantly repeated, or *would be generally known by readers of the time*, is not footnoted. Details—dates, specific facts, exact terms—and of course all quotations require footnotes. Actually, a good deal of the writing here will be in the form of transitional sentences and background information and thus will not require a footnote. I urge students to footnote in terms of the individual sentence rather than attempt an all-inclusive footnote at the end of a paragraph.

Content footnotes are often required to define terms and include peripheral material. I require at least one content footnote, and many of these are as interesting as items included in the body of the

paper. Also, content footnotes can be used to help explain vast shifts in time between events in a case. Bibliographies are somewhat easier to construct, but to avoid padding I ask that they be called "Working Bibliographies" and only stories *actually consulted and used* be included. (I require a minimum of twenty-five sources.)

Constructing Conclusions

Because these kinds of topics are often open-ended, I ask students to devote the last two pages to their own views of the case. Was justice done? What mistakes were made? Did they find the right man? In short, as the world's expert on this case, each student must present an opinion on what happened. In unsolved cases I ask students to construct a solution, and these are often ingenious and convincing. In fact, I'm sure some of my students have solved some nineteenth century murders (just as Edgar Allan Poe claimed he did)! Perhaps because we live in an age that believes in conspiracy, I get a great number of solutions that reflect this trend, but actually any summary that shows thought receives praise. During the last two weeks of the course I have each student give a brief oral report on his/her case, and at that time conclusions usually come under attack and require a good defense. I have found that the other students seem particularly interested in this phase of the course, and it's the only experience I can remember when students actually listen to their colleagues deliver an oral report. Professor Chris Madigan of Virginia Commonwealth University has his students play defense or prosecuting attorney in an oral presentation/summation to the rest of the class or jury. He reports that he is pleased with some of the questions classmates ask, although the student usually has no trouble getting the verdict desired.

The Final Check

About a week before papers are due, I hand out "A Ten Point Research Paper Checklist for Students" (see sample). The "points" stress the form of the paper—footnotes, bibliography, quotations, etc., and for the most part are a review of material that has been covered previously. Going over these details before handing the paper in usually reduces the number of careless and "nit-picking" errors that so often blemish an otherwise good paper. Most students, having spent a good deal of time and energy on these papers, are eager to make the final product as perfect as possible.

A TEN POINT RESEARCH PAPER CHECKLIST FOR STUDENTS

1. Footnotes are numbered correctly and all commas are correct. <u>Dates and page numbers are accurate</u>. At least <u>one</u> content footnote should appear. At least one source besides the <u>New York Times</u> should be used if at all possible.

2. The bibliography is correct—reverse indentation, periods after titles, newspapers underlined, alphabetical order, etc.

3. Quotations are accurate and introduced by verbs other than "said." Where possible your own words are fused within quotations and colons and semi-colons are used where needed. Brackets, ellipsis, and "sic" are used to make quotations more "streamlined."

4. The date of your case is mentioned at various points in the paper, not just your introduction.

5. Attempts have been made to include the physical description of people, their position, background, etc. The paper has a "personal" touch.

6. No "you's" or "I's" in the body of the paper. The paper is written in the past tense.

7. The paper is written in your words, your own style—rather than just changing a few words from the <u>New York Times</u>; the paper is a complete rewriting.

8. The paper is well organized and easy for a reader to follow without becoming lost in a mass of detail.

9. The last two pages set forth your own analysis of the case.

10. Final copy is in a folder, has been proofread carefully, and a carbon copy is included.

MISCHIEF AND MAYHEM

Some of my better student papers have been on shipwrecks, treasure hunts, Indian "uprisings," sports events, and assorted scandals. In general these are handled in the same way, but there are usually more magazine articles available. In the 1860s "Indians" are indexed in the "War" section, while in the 1870s the subject is placed under "Political." (Rather interesting in itself.) Although there are a few "happy ending" Indian stories, most of the cases recount how "hardy miners dispatched heathen savages,"and most students will be amazed to read about attitudes held during this period. In many ways these topics are more intriguing than murders, allowing students to be more creative in their papers. I have found that journalism students in particular like these kinds of topics and handle them as they could a feature story. After all, not all murders are interesting after a certain point, and I am reminded of the comment from the student who worked on a dismemberment case and complained that after they found the parts of the body, the "case was pretty cut and dried."

I have also tried other approaches. One term I simply concentrated on one period in history—the 1920s. Our class "text" was Frederick Lewis Allen's *Only Yesterday*, and every student investigated a strange event during that wild period. (It seemed that for awhile I was awash, as it were, in bootleg alcohol.) On another occasion I simply asked for a history of what life was like in our area in a particular year in the nineteenth century. By using our microfilm files of old weekly county newspapers, students compiled some bizarre local histories—a kind of freaky *Foxfire*. Some students have written on their family histories, researched prior inhabitants of old houses, and taken events reported in the *London Times* from the eighteenth century to produce a kind of "Bicentennial Minutes" format about concerns of the time. Sports is another treasure trove of material, and a paper on the 1922 Princeton football season, for instance, works well as the "amazing Princeton princes go undefeated, untied, and undoubted."

I always keep a copy of each paper done and my office bulges with as many files as any big city police department. And although I never planned on it, I've become an expert on American murders since 1851, something that makes me more popular at cocktail parties. My point here is that this procedure for dealing with freshman research papers has a number of advantages, I think, and for those interested in trying it, I guarantee you'll never again be forced to read another dull and predictable paper. And this is a claim I have never found on the back of a college text on research paper writing.

AN ANNOTATED LIST OF TOPICS

What follows is a list of topics that have resulted in superior papers for me, the cream of about five hundred cases I have assigned in the last five years. Even when I assign them a second or third time, they prove expandable enough to allow students to come up with different conclusions, depending on the facts they choose to include or ignore. For the most part I have stayed away from topics that are the subjects of books, or chapters in books, because for all practical purposes it proves nothing when students "rewrite" them. In those cases where books do exist, there is still enough newspaper material to allow students to formulate their own theories.

Almost all of the following "Murder" entries can first be found under the heading "Murders" in the *New York Times Index*, although a few are listed under the name given. The date cited is the year the case begins, but some continue for more than ten years and have magazine articles that can be traced. Two recent books cite some of the cases mentioned here and I have indicated where this occurs. *Bloodletters and Badmen*, by Jay Robert Nash (New York: M. Evans and Co., 1973), is an interesting encyclopedia of "American Criminals from the Pilgrims to the Present" and I once used it as a class text. *A Pictorial History of Crime*, by Julian Symons (New York: Crown Publishers, 1966), is less complete but still interesting.

The topics listed under Indians, explorers, biography, and potpourri are all workable with the same general format, but these subjects allow students to explore in even greater depth. I might suggest that teachers select topics from scattered periods of time so students do not crowd over the same reels of microfilm. It might be best to take just two cases from a given period and reserve the others for a later semester.

Most of the following annotations were written by the students who researched the case. I asked them to write blurbs as though they were trying to entice people to see a movie. In cases done by students prior to last year, I have written the items based on their papers using key quotations. Some of these topics sound better than they are perhaps, but so do movie posters; I leave it to you and your students to decide.

I. MURDERS

1. The Sickles Tragedy—1859
   A New York Senator encounters his wife's lover outside a Washington hot-spot and cries: "You have dishonored my bed and family, you scoundrel, prepare to die!"

2. Mary Hill Murder—1868
   A man throws his mother-in-law out the window and then tries to blame his wife.

3. John Smedick Murder—1868
   A policeman is killed and his killer sentenced to die, "demonstrating that violence [cannot] prevail in this Republican Government." Somewhat run-of-the-mill but the period of history is interesting.

4. Benjamin Nathan Murder—1870
   One of the first crimes that makes New Yorkers think their streets are not safe. (An unsolved murder)

5. Edward H. Rulloff Burglary and Murder Case—1870
   Two store clerks are killed in a robbery and two of the robbers are drowned crossing a river in their escape. After a bizarre trial, E. H. Rulloff is convicted and hanged. (Case cited in *Bloodletters and Badmen*)

6. Avery D. Putnam Murder—1871
   A trolley car ride to church turns to terror when a drunken masher attacks. (A rather commonplace little murder.)

7. James Fisk Murder—1872

   The great railroad stock manipulator is shot to death in a hotel room by a man he tried to swindle. (Cited in *Bloodletters and Badmen*)

8. William J. Sharkey Case—1872

   A murder case involving an early New York gangster who escapes prison and heads for Cuba.

9. Charles Goodrich Murder—1873

   Kate Stoddard confesses to the crime, but other people seem to be better suspects.

10. Kelsey Tar and Feather Outrage—1873

    A rejected suitor is tarred and feathered by a group of the girl's friends, but the joke turns grim when six months later the man's body is fished out of the bay. (An unsolved case but there is a trial.)

11. John McKenna Murder—1874

    A minor political murder involving Tammany Hall figure Richard Croker.

12. James Noe Murder—1875

    A robbery becomes a homicide when two men attempt to steal a shipment of feathers.

13. Judge Chisolm Murder—1877

    A Mississippi lynching of a judge and his family because of "Northern sympathies."

14. Staten Island Mystery—1878

    A corpse of a young girl is identified after police boil her arm and check for an old bone fracture.

15. Mary Eliza Billings Murder—1878

    A shot through an open window kills a woman and the estranged husband is sought.

16. The C. A. Cobb, Jr., Poison Case—1878

    A wife and her lover buy six ounces of arsenic, thirteen grams of morphine, and ten grams of strychnine for "medicinal purposes."

17. Richard Harrison Smith Murder—1878

    A policeman is murdered in his bed and "offended criminals" are questioned. However, in a curious incident, "the man's dog which was noted for barking whenever a stranger came near was quiet all night." The wife is brought to trial.

18. Mary Stannard Murder Case—1878

    A young pregnant girl is found dead and the chief suspect is "a lay preacher in a denomination of Christians which does not permit its teachers to be fathers of bastards." (Unsolved case but there is a trial)

19. Judge Elliot Murder—1879

    A Kentucky judge is shot by Col. Henry Buford, "who since the war continued to exercise his chivalrous propensities at odd times."

20. Jane Hull Murder—1879

    "An amateur detective in the person of a Boston journalist procure[s] the arrest of the guilty party." (Somewhat open and shut.)

21. Jennie Cramer's Mysterious Death—1881

    Was "the Belle of New Haven" an arsenic eater or did her boyfriend poison her?

22. Lamson-John Murder—1881

    A doctor gives his wealthy brother-in-law medicine that results in his death.

23. Captain A. C. Nutt and Nicholas Dukes Murders—1882

    A son avenges his father's death by killing "a crawling creature in Pennsylvania, Dukes by name, who, by a wicked perversion of law, escaped the gallows."

24. Rose Clark Ambler Murder—1883

    The Stratford mystery, as it was called, concerns an "infamous outrage" and fickle lover. (Unsolved case.)

25. The Rahway Mystery—1887

    Her tombstone read: "Cruelly Slain, A Woman and a Stranger, aged about 25 years." (Unsolved case)

26. Dr. P. H. Cronin—1889

    The treasurer of an Irish-American Organization is found dead after discovering some missing funds.

27. Helen Potts Murder—1891

    A student at Miss Day's Finishing School is found poisoned and suspicion falls upon "a conscientious medical student and a young man of the greatest honor."

28. Blanche Lamont Murder—1895

    The bodies of two girls are found in the Emanuel Baptist Church and Theodore Durrant is eventually hanged. A famous case cited in *Bloodletters and Badmen* and other books.

29. Josephine Barnaby Murder—1891

    A bottle of poison whiskey kills two women and an unscrupulous doctor is brought to light.

30. Meyer's Insurance Murder (Baum)—1893

    A doctor's wife "would go to live with a man as his wife, an insurance policy would be taken out, then death would soon follow."

31. Robert Ross Murder—1894

    An election day political murder on the streets of New York City. (A pedestrian case.)

32. Mrs. Henry H. Bliss Murder—1895

    A daughter serves her mother poisoned clam chowder, but a jury believes otherwise.

33. Benjamin Pitzel Murder—1895

    The last crime committed by the infamous H. H. Holmes who once held the Guinness record for most murders. A new book just published on Holmes tells about his Chicago murder castle and he is cited in *Bloodletters and Badmen* and *A Pictorial History of Crime*.

34. The Murder of William Guldensuppe—1897

    Some boys finds pieces of a man's body dismembered

by his straying wife and her fiendish lover. Thousands attend the viewing at which the body is laid out in a beautiful suit and no head. (Mentioned in *Bloodletters and Badmen*)

35. Emeline Reynolds Murder—1898

    A girl goes to the big city to study opera but is found dead in a man's hotel room. (An unsolved crime)

36. Kate Adams Murder—1898

    Poisoned bromo seltzer kills the wrong person. A case mentioned in *Bloodletters and Badmen* and *A Pictorial History of Crime*.

37. William Marsh Rice—1900

    A retired millionaire dies mysteriously and a strange will surfaces. Case mentioned in *A Pictorial History of Crime*.

38. Frank Young Murder—1904

    A Floradora girl shoots her sugardaddy.

39. William E. Annis Murder—1908

    The victim is shot by Peter Hains, Jr. while his brother, Thorton, uses a gun to hold members of the Bayside Yacht Club . . . at bay. A crime of passion involving the "unwritten law."

40. Lt. Guiseppe Petrosino Murder—1909

    A detective investigating the Black Hand is murdered. The first documentation of Mafia influence in America.

41. Ocey Snead Murder Case—1909

    A young boy found drowned in a bathtub leads police to the depraved Wardlaw sisters—a case mentioned in *Bloodletters and Badmen*.

42. Avis Linnell Murder Case—1911

    An innocent young girl goes to the big city and, alas, meets the wrong kind of man. She is found poisoned from cyanide of potassium and a Reverend Richeson is suspected.

43. Louise Beattie Murder—1911

    On a highway in Richmond, Virginia, a "stranger" shoots the wife of a prominent banker, but the gun mysteriously turns up in the husband's home.

44. Herman Rosenthal Murder—1912

    Often called the Becker Case, this murder was called "one of the most infamous and brazen crimes in this country's criminal annals." Mentioned in *Bloodletters and Badmen* and *A Pictorial History of Crime*.

45. Mrs. William Bailey Murder—1914

    A jealous wife shoots one of her husband's patients.

46. Barnett Baff Murder—1914

    The New York "chicken king" is killed in a struggle between poultry dealers.

47. The Death of Gaston Calmette—1914

    A Paris woman revenges newspaper attacks on her husband by killing the editor.

48. Dr. C. Franklin Mohr Murder Case—1915

    Was Dr. Mohr shot by two men who tried to rob him, or did his wife have him killed to inherit his fortune? (A rather short case)

49. Charles Murray Murder—1915

    A New York "Jack the Ripper" prowls the streets. A short unsolved case, but intriguing. He may have appeared again in 1916.

50. Elizabeth Nichols Murder—1915

    A wealthy widow is strangled and a two-year manhunt covers three states.

51. Arthur Warren Waite Murder—1916

    A man sets out to kill his wife and her family using arsenic, ground glass, influenza germs, a nasal spray of tubercular bacilli, and chloroform. A case mentioned in *A Pictorial History of Crime*.

52. Daniel Kaber Murder—1919

    In Lakewood, Ohio, a man is stabbed twenty-four times and at the autopsy they find enough arsenic "in his internal organs to kill four or five men." The wife says only that she hired men to pose as ghosts to drive out her husband's evil spirits.

53. F. R. Andrews Murder Case—1916

    A poisoning in the Archer House for Elderly People touches off an investigation involving an insane owner and rumors about other inmate deaths.

54. Mrs. Walter Wilkins Murder—1919

    A doctor claims robbers killed his wife, but he is accused of the murder.

55. Camillo Ciazzo Murder—1921

    A gang "forces" a man to commit murder, but the dead man's ghost leads him to confess. An early "syndicate" killing involving previous murders.

56. Luther Boddy Case—1922

    A man shoots a policeman in a celebrated case of police brutality.

57. West End Bank Messenger Robbery—1923

    Two bank messengers are killed and $43,000 stolen in a daring subway holdup.

58. The Strange Death of William Nelson McClintock—1924

    A millionaire orphan dies after eating poisoned oysters and a bacteriologist is suspected.

59. Dr. William Lilliendahl Murder—1927

    The wife tells a terrifying story of an assault by two blacks, but then a secret lover is found.

60. Grace Budd Murder—1928

    One of the nation's most grisly crimes. The depraved Albert Fish is convicted of murder and cannibalism.

61. Alfred Lingle Murder—1930

    A newspaper reporter is killed and it is discovered he had gangster connections.

62. The Eugenia Cedarholm Mystery—1930
A young heiress disappears and Edward Hall begins selling her estate.

63. The 3X Murders (Mozynski)—1930
A mysterious slayer sends letters to police and the papers stating he is a member of the Russian Red Diamond League in search of secret papers.

64. The Death of Zachary Smith Reynolds—1932
A shooting at the home of the wealthy tobacco heir could have been suicide or murder. A determined sheriff brings the wife to trial.

65. E. A. Ridley Murder Case—1933
A wealthy real estate owner, "Old Ridley—as he was called by the East Side folk near his cellar office— might have stepped straight out of the pages of Dickens." But then he and his secretary are found shot to death.

66. Samuel Drukman Murder—1935
This second degree murder is almost incidental to a political scandal which lasts six years. Bribery and obstruction of justice charges become so prevalent that the state supreme court asks for the resignation of the District Attorney.

67. Walter Liggett Murder—1935
The editor of the newspaper *The Mid-West American* is assassinated because of his attempts to clean up vice in Hennepin County, Minnesota.

68. Peter Levine Kidnapping—1938
After 94 days the decapitated kidnap victim is washed ashore on Long Island. To this day the case is unsolved and remains highly confidential—the student working on this topic was herself questioned by the FBI who wanted to know her interest in the matter.

69. Philadelphia Poisoning Ring—1939
"For three hundred dollars and upward a witch's broth and complete murder instructions were given to greedy, dissatisfied wives who had their husbands insured for a minimum of one thousand dollars."

70. Mrs. Wayne Lonergan Murder—1943
A soldier returns from the service and murders his wife. (Somewhat open and shut)

71. Sir Harry Oakes Murder—1943
Wealthy man murdered in his bed in the Bahamas— a famous unsolved case with more newspaper and magazine articles available than any student can read.

72. The Willie Earle Lynching—1947
A black man is dragged from a South Carolina jail by a group of angry cab drivers.

73. Janet Fay Murder—1949
The story of the sordid "lonely hearts" murders. A film was done on this case.

74. The Case of the Trenton Six—1951
A grocer misidentifies six black youths in a murder case because "they all look alike."

75. Pennsylvania Turnpike Murders—1953
A maniac kills two truck drivers and wounds another on one of America's major highways.

76. Charles Bates Murder—1953
A sailor is brutally beaten to death and Paul Pfeffer is sentenced to death—then another man confesses to the crime.

77. The Brooklyn Teenage Killers—1954
Four youths involved in a thrill killing.

78. Judge Chillingworth Murder—1955
A Florida judge and his wife disappear and years later the story is revealed.

79. Joseph Aronowitz Murder Case—1955
Murder and a western shoot out in the center of New York City.

80. Emmitt Till Case—1955
The famous case of a black youth shot for whistling at a white woman in Mississippi. A book has been written on this murder.

81. Michael Farmer Murder—1957
A teenage street gang kills a young boy.

82. Dr. John Bodkin Adams Case—1957
An English doctor is accused of killing his patients.

83. The Murder of Barbara Finch—1959
A famous case involving a respected doctor and his mistress. Many magazine articles here.

84. The Starved Rock Murders (Mrs. Robert Lindquist, et al.)—1960
A hiking trip in an Illinois State Park ends in murder. (A brief case)

85. The Bluebelle Yacht Case—1961
The story of a mysterious wreck at sea and "a mass murder by a berserk man."

86. Wylie-Hoffert Murder—1963
A case cited in books, magazines, and articles that became the basis for the first Kojak television movie.

87. Reuben Markowitz Murder—1963
A wealthy gambler tries to cover his World Series losses by murdering his bookie.

88. Alice Crimmins Case—1965
The murder of two children results in the mother's arrest. A recent book published on this case.

89. Judith Kavanaugh Murder—1966
Two murders linked to a counterfeit ring result in charges of "conduct unbecoming a lawyer" against F. Lee Bailey.

90. The Murder of Captain McDonald's Family—1970
Did three "hippies" invade an army base or did the officer himself slaughter his wife and children?

II. Indians

1. The First Sioux Uprising—1862
    "The brutal savages passed a stick through both ankles of a woman and dragged her over the prairie, till from that alone, torn and mangled, she died."

2. The Career of General Hancock, Indian Fighter—1867
    The Beau Brummel of the plains brings the Indians to the treaty table.

3. Spotted Tail, Indian Chief—1869-1880s
    A great Sioux leader directs his tribe both on the field and at the negotiating table in the war against the white man.

4. The Piegan Indian Slaughter—1870
    A tribe of Blackfoot Indians is wiped out by soldiers, and settlers fear "they will not be satisfied without that revenge that an Indian naturally craves."

5. The Modoc Indian War—1872
    Led by Shark Nasty Jim, the Modocs strike back at soldiers trying to put them on a reservation.

6. The Cheyenne Indian Uprising—1874-1878
    The prelude to Little Big Horn.

7. The Nez-Percé Indian War—1877
    "The only good Indian is a dead Indian," is how the government looked at the Nez-Percé Indian War in 1877. Chief Joseph leads his tribe in a 120-day war against the United States cavalry.

8. The Ute Indian Uprising—1879
    "The Indian agent decided it would be good for the Utes to become farmers, and having come to this decision, it was perfectly immaterial to him that the Utes preferred to live by hunting."

9. Poncas Indian Controversy—1879
    "Persecution, trickery, and injustice" by the white man as the Indians are "relocated."

III. Explorers

1. The Search for Sir John Franklin—1856
    An expedition to find the Northwest Passage disappears amid many speculations.

2. Captain Hall's Arctic Expedition—1871
    A search for the missing Sir John Franklin results in a strange death.

3. Salomon Andree Arctic Expedition—1897
    A polar voyage ends in tragedy.

4. Captain Robert F. Scott's Antarctic Expedition—1912
    An early journey to the South Pole ends in tragedy amid "the eternal silence of the great white desert."

5. Alf Wegener Greenland Expedition—1930
    A German expedition led by a famed explorer results in death.

6. Dr. Lincoln Ellsworth Flight Expedition—1935
    A plane flight across the Antarctic in which two men are missing for eight weeks as they cover 1,700 miles of frozen wasteland.

IV. Biography

1. The Career of Louis Kossuth—1851-1894
    A Hungarian statesman comes to America to "procure aid for his revolutionary propagandism."

2. The Career of John Mitchel and the Slavery Question—1853
    An inspiring story of how one man stirs up emotions in order to hold on to everything he believes.

3. The Career of Victoria Woodhull—1870
    An early leader in the suffrage movement who believed in spiritualism and free love.

4. The Stormy Career of Reverend T. DeWitt Talmage, Evangelist—1879
    After his wife's strange death the congregation tries to replace him.

5. Richard Hobson, the Hero of Santiago Bay—1899
    A hero of the Spanish-American War encounters rough times in civilian life.

6. Emilio Aquinaldo, The Hero of the Philippine Insurrection—1899
    A patriot leads his people against the U. S. Marines.

7. The Boxing Career of Jack Johnson—1910-1915
    The first black heavyweight champion in his bouts against the "white hopes."

8. The Career of Owen Madden—1914-1964
    One of the few prohibition gangsters to retire to Hot Springs after an illustrious career. (Cited in *Bloodletters and Badmen*.)

9. The Ordeal of Jeremiah O'Leary—1915
    A man tries to persuade America to avoid war with Germany but becomes a fugitive for his actions against the United States.

10. Battling Siki, Boxer—1922
    "From the jungles of West Africa came a man with the mentality of a backward toad . . . but the soul of a god."

11. Kid Chocolate, Boxer—1928
    A classy featherweight shoots for the title.

12. The Bullfighting Career of Sidney Franklin—1929
    The only American bullfighter to make it big in Spain. His fights were broadcast on the radio in this country.

13. The Criminal Career of Jack "Legs" Diamond—1929-1931
    The famous gangster and his friends make news until gunmen catch up to him in a hotel room.

14. The Criminal Career of Arthur Flegenheimer—1931
Dutch Schultz, from beer runner to gang lord. A book has been published on his life.

15. The Religious Career of Father Divine—1930
A "messenger from God" offers paradise to those who give him all their worldly goods.

16. The Boxing Career of Primo Carnera—1930–1936
The circus strong man whom gangsters promoted to world champion. Sports reporters never tired of making fun of him.

17. The Saga of Winnie Ruth Judd—1931–1971
The famous trunk murderess keeps escaping from prison. Recent book published on her life.

18. The Trials of Fritz Kuhn—1936–1949
A leader of the German-American Movement meets rough opposition when war breaks out.

19. Harry Bridges, Labor Leader—1938–1952
The struggle of early labor unions is dramatized by an attempt to deport one of its early organizers.

V. Potpourri

1. The Sayer-Heenan Boxing Match—1860
An English bout that ends in a near riot.

2. Sir Roger Charles Tichborne Identity Case—1871
The case used as the basis of numerous fictional stories of impersonation from Mark Twain's time to today. An enormous amount of material here and a few books.

3. The James H. Ingersoll Forgeries—1872
Boss Tweed and Company build a new court house.

4. Hank Smith, Swindler—1872
A Tammany Hall police commissioner cheats the city.

5. The Henry Ward Beecher-Theodore Tilton Trial—1873
A famous minister is accused of adultery.

6. Brigham Young's Divorce—1875
The famed Mormon leader is sued for divorce by his twenty-sixth wife.

7. Mountain Meadow Massacre—1877
Brutal murders of men, women and children, kept secret for over 15 years, damage the Mormon faith. Books have been written on this topic.

8. The Wreck of the Metropolis—1878
A steamship breaks apart at sea with great loss of life.

9. The Johnstown Flood—1889
The day the dam broke and caused one of Pennsylvania's greatest tragedies.

10. The James H. Edgar "Suicide" Case—1890
A brazen swindler seeks unclaimed bodies to collect an inheritance.

11. Robert Thorpe Murder and Riot—1900
The murder of a policeman leads to "racial incidents." The *New York Times* believed "the cause of all the trouble [was] that many negroes who live on money supplied by women are so dangerous that they incite the rest of them to riot."

12. Dynamite Conspiracy—1912
The defendants claim "killing is not murder if done in a class war."

13. Dr. Friedrich Franz Friedmann's Tuberculosis Treatment—1913
A German scientist becomes a millionaire with a "secret formula" derived from turtles.

14. Clara Ellert Rape and Scandal—1914
A city administration is disgraced.

15. Grover Cleveland Bergdoll Draft Case—1914–1944
A man hides in his mother's house to escape World War I and weaves a fantastic story of buried gold in the Maryland mountains.

16. The Shooting of J. P. Morgan—1915
A crazed gunman goes after the wealthy philanthropist.

17. The Controversy Surrounding the Film *Birth of a Nation*—1915
Hollywood's first great movie seems to promote the Ku Klux Klan.

18. Edith Cavell Spy Case—1915
An English woman is executed for helping people flee Belgium in World War I.

19. The Movies Go To War—1916
Hollywood is motivated to "make stronger soldiers, stir patriotism, and create prejudice against the Kaiser." Cast of thousands.

20. The Movie Censorship Campaign—1919
Too much sex and violence on the screen brings a crackdown.

21. The Fatty Arbuckle Scandal—1921
A starlet is found "crushed to death" at a wild Hollywood party and the 350-pound film comedian is brought to trial. A famous case.

22. James A. Stillman Divorce Case—1921
A bizarre trial of co-respondents and suits and countersuits among the 1920's beautiful people.

23. Izzy Einstein and Moe Smith, Prohibition Agents—1922
"They're not a bit slow and never take dough,/They change their appearance where ever they go,/Wonderful fellows are Izzy and Moe."

24. The Antigonish Ghost (Prince)—1922
Unexplained fires, noises, and strange occurrences take place in a sparsely inhabited valley deep in the woods and mountains of Nova Scotia.

25. Earl Carroll and the Bathtub Party Case—1926
A wild theatre party with the host serving bootleg

alcohol from a bathtub in which a nude chorus girl is immersed. Shocking!

26. The controversy over the play *Green Pastures*—1930
Was this drama deeply religious, blasphemous, racist, or a humble view of how blacks envision "De Lawd"?

27. John J. O'Connell, Jr., Kidnap Case—1933
A wealthy brewery owner is abducted by "the nation's last organized kidnapping ring."

28. Donald L. Robinson Disappearance—1937
Spies, forged documents, and fraudulent passports in Stalin's Russia on the eve of World War II.

29. The College Basketball Scandals—1951
Crooked gamblers invade the campus.

AUTHOR

W. Keith Kraus

Mr. Kraus received a Ph.D. at Southern Illinois University and is presently Professor of English at Shippensburg State College, Pennsylvania. He previously taught at Northville (Michigan) High School and at Northern Iowa University. In 1975, Mr. Kraus was awarded the Commonwealth of Pennsylvania Distinguished Teaching Chair for his method of using old newspaper accounts of murder cases as subjects for freshman research papers.